LEFT BEHIND AT ZEEBRUGGE

The Incredible Story of
Sergeant Harry Wright DSM MSM RMLI

A Personal Account of the Raid on Zeebrugge
And his Experiences as a WW1 Prisoner of War

By
Sergeant Harry Wright DSM MSM RMLI

Editor of First Edition
Captain Derek Oakley MBE RM

Editor of Second Edition and Series Editor
Colonel B L Carter OBE RM

Left behind at Zeebrugge
Copyright © Royal Marines Historical Society 2017

All Rights Reserved

All rights reserved. No part of this publication may be reproduced, distributed, or transmitted in any form or by any means, including photocopying, recording, or other electronic or mechanical methods, without the prior written permission of the publisher, except in the case of brief quotations embodied in critical reviews and certain other non-commercial uses permitted by copyright law. For permission requests, write to the publisher, addressed "Attention: Honorary Editor" at the address below.

ISBN 978-1-908123-15-2

First published in 1990 as 'Memoirs of Sgt Harry Wright (Zeebrugge & Aftermath)' by the
ROYAL MARINES HISTORICAL SOCIETY
Royal Marines Museum
Eastney
Southsea
Hants PO4 9PX
United Kingdom

Second Edition published in 2017

Cover, design and layout
Tim Mitchell
www.tim-mitchell.co.uk

Printed and bound in Great Britain by
CPI Antony Rowe Ltd, Chippenham and Eastbourne

Sergeant Harry Wright DSM MSM RMLI

Contents

1	Zeebrugge	3
2	Bruges	17
3	Cortrai	27
4	Dendermonde	35
5	Dülman	43
6	Cottbus	59
7	Brandenberg	67

Preface

by Captain Derek Oakley MBE RM

This special publication has been compiled from three hand-written diaries kept by PLY 12433 Colour Sergeant Harry Wright DSM, MSM, mainly whilst he was a prisoner of war after the raid on Zeebrugge. The diaries were written after his return to England from shorthand notes he kept in camp. This accounts for a difference of tense from time to time. As far as possible I have faithfully reproduced his own words, except the very occasional misspelling, and minor changes where the original was not entirely clear.

Harry Wright was born in 1889 and joined the Royal Marines Light Infantry in 1906. In the early part of World War One, as an acting Lance Sergeant he was transferred from *HMS Cumberland* to *HMS Astroea* for service ashore in the Cameroons, then German South West Africa, where he was 'favourably noted for these operations.' He served as a signalman alongside the French Senegalese forces during the fighting at Kribi. He then saw service with the Royal Naval Division on the Western Front.

He volunteered for the 4th Battalion and was the Platoon Sergeant of number 10 Platoon of Plymouth Company at the raid on Zeebrugge for which he was awarded the DSM. These memoirs cover the assault and his subsequent capture by the Germans, one of only fourteen Royal Marines to be left behind.

Colour Sergeant Wright was recalled for service at the outbreak of World War Two at the age of 50 and served mostly in DEMS (Defensively Equipped Merchant Ships). He was torpedoed and bombed several times, spent days in open boats at sea, and yet survived to tell the tale.

During the 1950's he wrote many articles for The Globe & Laurel and other magazines such as The British Legion Journal and his local Parish magazine at Hextable, near Swanley in Kent.

I had the privilege of meeting Harry Wright when I was editor of The Globe & Laurel and he immediately struck me as a story teller par excellence. His highly perceptive and retentive memory, coupled with an intricate attention to detail, made him a social historian as well as a military one. He was one of 'old breed', passionately loyal to the Corps he served for so long and with such distinction. He died on the 4th May 1976 at the age of 87, and these memoirs will now stand as a lasting memorial to this Old Soldier.

(Note by Editor of this Second Edition: this SP was originally published as 'Memoirs of Sgt Harry Wright (Zeebrugge & Aftermath)'. When it came to republishing this remarkable story I felt that the title belied the enormity of his achievements, hence the change of title and restyling. Some of the photographs are of poor quality and having handwritten captions, but I felt it was still worth using them in the interests of provenance.)

Zeebrugge

After six weeks hard training at Deal, the 4th Battalion Royal Marines received orders to proceed to a certain destination. We had during this time been inspected by HM King George V, The First Lord of the Admiralty and the Adjutant General of the RM Corps. The latter informed us that what we were going to do would live in history for ever and he hoped that each man would do his duty and uphold the honour of the Royal Marines whose fame was known all over the world. Any man who did not want to go had the privilege of falling out, but as no-one accepted the offer, we all became volunteers. We had been informed that we were going to France and each man had been kitted up with all the necessary fighting gear which every British 'Tommy' carries when proceeding overseas.

On April 6th at 6am the Battalion fell in and was inspected by our Colonel, Lt Col B N Elliot, and with the band leading, we marched off through the town to the station. The people of Deal turned out to give us a good send off. No-one ever witnessed a happier lot of men; we were all singing, laughing or joking, and as we passed our old bayonet instructor 'who had given us a stiff training' we gave him a rousing cheer. There was a special train in the station and the whole battalion of some 850 Officers and men were entrained in less than 10 minutes. As we left the band played 'Should Auld Acquaintance', etc, and the boys sang in return. In a short time we steamed into Dover station where a steamer was waiting for us and this convinced us that we were going to France. We were soon on board, all of us going down below having had strict orders to do so. The Captain of the steamer shouts down from the bridge to our Colonel *"Am I to proceed direct to France?"* In reply the Colonel said *"Proceed to sea and I will then give you your orders."* On getting to sea the Captain was given sealed orders, and on breaking the seal and reading them he at once turned his ship to port and proceeded towards Sheerness.

When we arrived there we were rather surprised to read a signal from one of the ships which said that A and B Companies will proceed to *HMS Hindustan* and C Company to *HMS Vindictive*. Two tugs were sent to the steamer, the men for *Hindustan* going on one, and the men for *Vindictive* on the other. On getting alongside the *Vindictive* we were surprised to see how she was fitted up. There was a special deck built on the port side with ramps leading from the lower deck on the starboard side up to the special deck. On the port side there were 14 huge gangways pointing out to sea and triced up with pulleys ready for dropping. She carried two 11" howitzers, one forward, one aft, numerous Stokes guns and a pom-pom in the crow's nest half way up the mast, the majority of her armament being on the port side. Sandbag revetments were built around the forebridge and other vital parts. In addition there were two very powerful flame-throwers and machine guns.

As regards ammunition the ship must have been a floating arsenal for there were shells already fused everywhere. The ship carried her proper complement for sea and with C Company comprising some 270 men, we were rather overcrowded; but we were all staid men used to roughing it in all parts of the world, so this little inconvenience was nothing to us and we soon settled down.

The next day Captain A F B Carpenter RN had everybody aft on the Quarterdeck and told us for the first time what we were going to do. *"We are going"* he said *"on a very dangerous errand, and any hitch in the operation might mean a naval disaster, so it is everyone's duty to do his best. The Vindictive is going through the enemy's minefields and alongside the mole at Zeebrugge. On getting there the 4th Battalion will storm the mole and engage the enemy while at the same time, three blockships filled with concrete, will go round the other side of the mole and sink themselves in the mouth of the canal. A bridge connects the mole with Zeebrugge and during the operation a submarine with 10 tons of high explosive will be set under the bridge and so cut off reinforcements from Zeebrugge. While this is going on two other ships will proceed to Ostend and sink themselves in the mouth of the canal there, and by this means close up the hornet's nest of submarines so that none can come out and those that are out, cannot go back to refit. It may so happen"* he continued *"that some of you may have the misfortune to be captured; if so, bear in mind you must not give any information to the enemy, especially about our fleet, but on the other hand there is certain information we would like you to pass on. In the first place tell them that we are capturing their submarines, taking them to England, putting English crews onboard and sending them to sea again as decoys. Secondly tell them that on every merchant ship there is fitted an instrument which can detect a submarine at a 2 mile radius. This information must be tactfully passed on, but let the enemy bring the subject up first."* Captain Carpenter finished by saying *"The success of this whole operation depends on two things namely secrecy, and the wind, which must be blowing towards the enemy so that the destroyers can use their smokescreens effectually."*

The Marines were now taken by their officers, one platoon at a time, and shown a clay model of the mole, which was 1800 yards long and 80 yards wide. It was built in peacetime to enable ships to land their passengers as the water was too shallow inshore. The passengers could be landed either side according to the tide. There was a railway running the whole length of the mole to take passengers to Zeebrugge. On the sea end of the mole was a lighthouse. Since it had been taken over by the Germans the mole had been fortified, being one mass of concrete shelters. In the centre was a huge seaplane shed with six powerful machine guns. On the sea end of the mole and about 50 yards from the lighthouse was a strong concrete shelter with four 5" guns and machine guns were hidden in various places along the mole. *Vindictive* would go alongside the mole on the northern side. Grappling irons would then be lowered onto the concrete wall, and on a given signal, the first Company would land.

We had previously drawn lots to see who should land first and C Company, all Plymouth marines, won that honour. Each Company had four platoons, Plymouth Company being numbered 9, 10, 11 & 12. Some sailors, as demolition party,

View from the land end of the Mole, Zeebrugge, Belgium, c1918. © Trustees of the National Museum of the Royal Navy

A close up of the Mole at Zeebrugge, Belgium, 1918. © Trustees of the National Museum of the Royal Navy.

would accompany the leading company. On the advance being sounded 9 & 10 Platoons would land first, turn to the right on getting ashore and capture the first objective which was supposed to be a strong point 200 yards along the mole. Almost immediately afterwards 11 & 12 Platoons and seamen would land, turn to the left and advance towards the four guns and capture them. At the same time, if the enemy extinguished the lighthouse, they would burn a flare so that the blockships could get their bearings; the operation was to be carried out at 12 midnight. On reaching their positions the platoon sergeants of the leading platoons would fire red flares into the air as a signal for the other company to come onshore. They would land, come through our line, carrying objectives to a depth of 800 yards, and then, on firing their red flares, 1, 2, 3, & 4 Platoons of the Chatham marines would come through the others already in position on the mole and carry objectives to a depth of one mile.

Each platoon was armed with a Lewis gun and a flame thrower. There was also a special platoon of machine gunners and a special signals platoon with telephones, etc. There were also demolition parties for blowing up the concrete shelters and sheds. Each man carried Mills grenades and every NCO had a stunning mallet for close fighting. The officers carried revolvers and walking out canes weighted with lead on the handle end. Each platoon had two ladders and four ropes, for on landing, there was a drop of 4' from the gangway to the concrete wall; then from this ledge there was a sheer drop of 20', hence the use of ladders and ropes. The signal to retire would be a succession of short blasts on the *Vindictive's* siren, when the Chatham's marines would retire first, followed by the Portsmouth marines and then the Plymouth Company embarking last. All the wounded and dead to be taken aboard first.

We were to take our positions at all costs and to destroy everything we came into contact with. Each man wore an India rubber swimming belt under his tunic in case he fell into the sea. The demolition parties, chiefly sailors, carried ammanol, gun-cotton, safety and instantaneous fuzes and detonators. The Howitzers and pom-pom guns were manned by The Royal Marine Artillery, in three reliefs; and the Stokes guns and machine guns manned by the marine infantry, they would keep up a covering fire while we were ashore. Each platoon had a specially trained bombing section to deal with dugouts etc. The monitors out at sea would assist us by trying to silence the batteries at Zeebrugge. The enemy thinking this an attempt to take Zeebrugge would concentrate their fire on to the mole and so give the blockships a chance to get in. Aeroplane photographs were handed round to the officers and NCO's and some of us drew a sketch from the photograph marking off the positions. I think I am right in saying that, by the time we had seen the model and drawn the sketch, the officers and NCO's could have at least walked from one end of the mole to the other blindfolded; and every man knew what to do and where to go.

All day Sunday we were busy detonating grenades and unloading tugs which came alongside with extra sandbags and shells. As each ship was unloaded she was sent to sea and given strict orders to stay there until given further orders. The men stripped to the waist and worked with a will finishing late that night with everyone dead tired. We had a good supper and turned into our hammocks for the night.

On Monday 8th April during the forenoon it was reported by wireless from the Belgian coast that the wind was favourable and it was decided to do the 'stunt' at midnight. The two companies of marines left the *Hindustan*, some coming on board *Vindictive* and others going on board *Iris* and *Daffodil*, two smaller ships. The destroyer *Warwick* with Vice Admiral Sir Roger Keyes came out from Dover and gave orders for our little fleet to proceed to Zeebrugge. At 11am we got under way towing *Iris* and *Daffodil*, Our fleet consisted of *Warwick*, *Vindictive* and five obsolete cruisers, *Intrepid*, *Brilliant*, *Iphigenia*, *Thetis* and *Sirius* filled with concrete. In addition there

No 10 Platoon of Plymouth Company at Deal before the Zeebrugge raid. Lt R G Stanton (centre) died of wounds before getting ashore, on his left is the Company Commander Maj B G Weller, who took command of the battalion when the CO and 2 i/c were killed. Sgt Harry Wright is seated, fourth from left.

were a number of motor boats and a submarine filled with high explosive. We also had an escort of destroyers to guard us from submarine attack. Flying overhead were a few aeroplanes.

It was a beautiful day and everyone was in high spirits. As we left harbour the *Hindustan* and other ships gave us a rousing cheer. We did not look a very imposing force as we got out to sea and out of sight of land. An organised attack by German destroyers and submarines could have easily put our little obsolete fleet to the bottom. We reached our destination late that night and lay just off Zeebrugge. The monitors and aeroplanes were already engaging the enemy. It was a very dark night and we could see the flashes of the guns ashore as they replied, and as we watched and listened the bombardment got more intense, until it seemed to us that nothing could land there and live. They certainly knew we were coming. A few quick flashes on the Morse lamps, just a single letter code, and our little fleet left again without being seen by the enemy. The men were very disappointed with the exception of those who understood. We could not hope to effect a surprise if the enemy were wide awake and prepared for us.

The cruiser HMS Vindictive, showing upper deck with wooden brows rigged for landing parties, before the raid on Zeebrugge, which took place on 23rd April 1918. © Trustees of the National Museum of the Royal Navy

We arrived back at Sheerness during the forenoon and the *Hindustan* detachments were sent over to her. During the afternoon Admiral Keyes came aboard the *Vindictive* we all fell in on the Quarterdeck. He mounted a bollard and said *"Well men, I am very sorry you were disappointed last night. In the first place the wind changed at the last moment making our smoke screen useless. Secondly, through the bombardment, the enemy had an idea that something was going to happen and would have been prepared for us. Zeebrugge itself is bristling with guns and had we attempted to land last night, it may easily have proved a naval disaster. To prove the accuracy of the German gunfire, one of our little fleet sent out a wireless message, the enemy could find her position and range by the sound of the wireless and dropped a shell close by."* The admiral concluded by saying *"Have patience, men, I can promise you a successful operation."* We gave him a rousing cheer as he left the ship.

We now had a wait of seven days because the wind would not blow in the proper direction. All this time we were in constant communication with our ships at Dunkirk who reported every day the direction of the wind. To kill time we went to physical drill, and sports were organised to keep the men fit. We also had orders to take the toe plates, heels and sprigs out of our boots so that we would not slip on the concrete mole. We also had lectures and practiced for the stunt; no one was allowed onshore and all our letters were drafted out for us. On having a favourable report from the Belgian coast our little fleet set sail once more for the operation but on getting half way there, the wind changed again and we were obliged once more to go back, much to the disgust of the men. The marines from the *Vindictive* now went to the *Hindustan* and another large ship was sent to accommodate the men as we were overcrowded. We had plenty of good food on the *Hindustan* and plenty of physical drill.

On Sunday 21st April the parson gave us a very interesting sermon on what became of one when we died. Little did we think that within a few hours so many brave lads would have laid down their lives. On Monday 22nd April we were drilling on the Quarterdeck when the signal came to prepare for the stunt. We went below, labelled our kitbags and other things we did not want, and handed them over to the ship's steward. A tug was already alongside to take us to the *Vindictive* and Colonel Elliot watched us as we clambered over the side. If anyone was downhearted and looked at our Colonel, they would at once feel happy and confident. There he stood, a fine specimen of manhood, wearing his DSO and Serbian decorations, and a smile on his face. The men loved him for he had a kind word for everyone, moreover he could get the last ounce of work out of NCO's and men under his command.

We crowded on board *Vindictive* and at 3pm we once again left for Zeebrugge, taking as usual *Iris* and *Daffodil* with the remainder of the Battalion in tow. Something seemed to tell us we were going in that night. At midnight it would be St George's Day, and when at sea, the Admiral made the signal which will always be remembered *"St George for England"* to which the Captain replied *"May we give the dragon's tail a damned good twist."* It was beautiful day and one could see miles out to sea, which was calm as a mill pond. The wind again seemed likely to change and signals were exchanged to that effect, but we kept steadily on course. We rendezvoused half way, where the fleet divided, three ships going to Ostend. The daily ration of rum was issued to the men about 8pm and the officers and platoon sergeants were made responsible that each man only had his share, and what was over was emptied down the scupper. Right up to the last the men were in good humour, laughing, joking and playing cards, just as if they were on leave. Some were boasting of what Jerry would get when they got on the mole.

The order was passed; everyone fell in on the upper deck fully rigged. Our little Sergeants Mess was crowded; we hastily shook hands and went out to get our men up, and then on the upper deck in the darkness and quiet. Rifles were loaded and bayonets fixed. There was a bit of a sea running and the ship made its way slowly through the water. The destroyers went ahead and put up a dense smoke screen. There were no lights showing and everyone talked in whispers. Our nerves were taut, almost to breaking point. Would we get alongside the mole without the enemy knowing? There we stood, rifles in our hands ready for the dash forward; not a movement, hardly a whisper and only the noise of the propellors broke the silence. Would we never get there? A starshell floated just above the ship, lighting it up as though it were day. One could see the men's white, drawn faces ready for the spring forward. No sooner had the light gone down than another went up. *"They've seen us"* someone whispered, for the lights had been fired from the mole.

We were crowded together, shoulder to shoulder as thick as bees, when the silence was broken by a terrific bang followed by a crash as the fragments of shell fell amongst us killing and maiming the brave fellows as they stood to their arms. The mole is in sight – we can see it off our port quarter, but too late. Our gunners replied to their fire, but they could not silence that terrible battery of 5" guns, now firing into the ship at a range of only 100 yards and from behind concrete walls. A very powerful searchlight was turned on us from Zeebrugge and the powerful batteries also fired upon us. The slaughter was terrible, Colonel Elliot and Major Cordner were killed by the same shell whilst in an exposed position on the bridge waiting to give the order 'advance'. The shells came onboard thick and fast for they could not miss such a large an object, but the brave fellows stuck to their post, only waiting their chance when the enemy would not have it all their own way. Men were hopping about on one leg, shouting in their frenzy. Some of the bodies were intermingled with the decks and our ranks got thinner every moment. They were taking every bit of cover they could.

"What was Captain Carpenter doing?" There he stood on the forebridge steadily giving orders to the engine room staff and doing his utmost to get the ship alongside, and as cool as if he was taking it alongside the mole in peacetime. Never did a man do a job more bravely. The guns crew of the *Vindictive* did their work splendidly. The pom-pom in the crow's nest had three crews wiped out but luckily the sergeant in charge was only wounded and remained at his post, the pom-pom kept going all the time. (This man, Sergeant Norman Finch got the VC and richly deserved it). At last we came alongside and by this time we were only 30 yards from the muzzles of the German guns. The grappling irons were dropped and officers tried to get ashore to make them fast, but as each one attempted it he was killed by machine gun fire. The *Iris* now came up on our starboard side and rammed *Vindictive* to the mole, and the gangways only two left out of fourteen were lowered on to the mole.

The cruiser HMS Vindictive at Dover, 24th April 1918 upon her return from the Zeebrugge Raid of the previous day. © Trustees of the National Museum of the Royal Navy

No sooner had this been done than the order to 'Advance' was given by Major Weller who had assumed command so the remnants of 9 & 10 Platoons lead the way up the ramp. My officer, Lieutenant Stanton, having been fatally wounded, I had the honour, as Platoon Sergeant, of leading 10 Platoon on shore. Up the ramp we dashed carrying our ladders and ropes. We passed over dead bodies lying everywhere and over big gaps made in the ship's decks by shell fire, finally crossing the remaining two gangways which were only just hanging together, and then jumping on to the concrete wall, only to find it swept with machine gun fire. Our casualties were so great that out of a platoon of 45 only 12 of us landed, and 9 Platoon led by Lieutenant Lamplough also had about that number. We hastily lowered our ladders and dropped on to the lower part of the mole and two men at once got down the 20' drop and rushed across to the shed on the far side. Everyone was anxious to get down as the machine guns were mowing our lads down. As some of us were getting down the ladders and ropes a few Germans rushed across the mole with bombs, but it was now our turn and not one of them got half way across.

We rallied the men, now reduced to no more than 14 in the two platoons, and charged our position. No one can imagine the feelings as we dashed forward, our rifles with a terrible grip, a fearful hatred on our faces and ready to plunge our bayonets into the first living creature that opposed us and so revenge our comrades lying dead on the *Vindictive*. But alas, on reaching our position we found the enemy had gone, retiring to their concrete shelters further up the mole. Disgusted we now turned our attention to the concrete dugouts on our right and left and gave them a good bombing, and as there was a German destroyer lying alongside the mole on our left, we bombed her also. The mole in the meantime was being swept by machine guns. The two platoon sergeants, Sergeant Bailey and myself now fired our red Very Lights to let the others know we had reached our position but the *Iris*, after pushing *Vindictive* in, went alongside the mole to land her marines. There were 56 onboard but the batteries ashore got a direct hit amongst them and 49 were killed and the others wounded. The casualties were so great amongst 11 & 12 Platoons, and with nearly all the sailors being killed, there were but a few to deal with the German guns, but what there were dashed for the guns only to be killed, Commander Brock amongst them. What few were left on the *Vindictive* came through our lines. These brave fellows, headed by their officers, came on walking in extended line as if they were on parade, but only a few of them reached their positions.

The Germans, in their excitement, had forgotten to extinguish the lighthouse so the blockships, taking a bearing from the light went around the other side of the mole, sank the German dredger on their way in, passed under the muzzles of the batteries ashore and sank themselves obliquely in the entrance of the canal, the crews, what few were left, getting away in their boats. The submarine C3 went under the bridge and blew herself up despite the fact that some German soldiers on the bridge tried to stop her with a machine gun. The explosion was so great that the whole concrete mole shook from end to end. A shell had struck *Vindictive's* siren so that she could not make the 'retire' signal, but another ship was ordered to make it.

The signal was made to retire after the *Vindictive* had been alongside for one hour, but instead of making a succession of short blasts, she made a succession of long and short blasts. We took it however, as the order to retire and commenced doing so, when an order was passed that it was not the signal to retire and we were ordered back to our position. We obeyed the order and very shortly afterwards we had the terrible ordeal of seeing our only means of escape slowly move away. The *Vindictive* had left, the officers thinking everyone was aboard. We were 200 yards from the ship when she left and we still had the 20' wall to climb.

We were now stranded, left to the tender mercy of the Huns, our only hope now gone. How hard it seemed to us, to think we had come through the terrible slaughter, to be alive and well and now no means of escape. Shells were now falling fast on the mole. How long would it be before death relieved us of this terrible agony of suspense? But wait, the motor boats would be sent in to our assistance and with this faint hope we crossed the mole and climbed the 20' wall, took our equipment off, blew up our swimming belts and waited, lying stiff and pretending to be dead. Some of us looked over the wall occasionally but not a vestige of anything was in sight. To remind us that we must not look over the wall a machine gun only 30 yards away was turned on us, but lying close to the concrete wall, it was not so effective as it might have been. For two hours we lay there and listened, with star shells floating over us, some falling and burning us. Two men were badly wounded but lay still for the sake of the others. Would relief never come? What would happen to us in the end?

The breach in the mole at the harbour of Zeebrugge, made by the submarine HMS C3, during the raid in 1918. © Trustees of the National Museum of the Royal Navy

A crane and a minesweeper on the Mole, Zeebrugge, Belgium, c1918. The crane was destroyed during the raid of 23rd April. © Trustees of the National Museum of the Royal Navy

The bridge of HMS Iris II after the raid on Zeebrugge, Belgium, 1918. © Trustees of the National Museum of the Royal Navy

Shells from our own ships were now striking the mole and we could hear them whistling overhead. The firing now eased down and a German officer and two privates came to us, shone a torch on us, and thinking we were a heap of dead, went away. It would have been useless to have killed them so we lay still. About half an hour after this the firing ceased and the Germans came out in force, walked along the mole to where we were lying. Some of them stooped down, no doubt to search the dead, when one man moved and then another. Nerves, being highly strung, they jumped back shouting and gesticulating, and made ready with their bayonets. We had not relinquished our rifles and got ready to fight to a finish if need be, to die fighting. A German officer shouted in quite good English *"The games up, lads"* and seeing that we still hesitated he continued *"Play the game and we will play the game with you. Lay down your arms and put your hands up and we will not harm you"* We obeyed this order and were made prisoners of war.

We were now searched and such things as clasp knives, swimming belts and whistles were taken off us and we were put into a concrete shelter with a guard over us. The two men who were wounded were medically treated and sent off to hospital. Whilst in the shelter we soon summed up how many were captured. There being Captain J M Palmer, 2 Sergeants, 1 Corporal and 10 Privates including the two wounded. All of us belonged to C Company Plymouth Division and the majority of the men from 9 & 10 Platoons whose duty it was to remain last on the mole. We saw the 5" guns, none of which were damaged. There had been steady rain all the time and we were wet through. Our faces were black from the smoke and dirt and we were feeling wretched.

A strong escort was sent to conduct us along the mole to another shelter and a large number of soldiers and sailors had by this time come out of their rat holes to have a look at us, following us up the mole grinning all over their faces. *"Look"* said one of them in English *"we sink three big English ships in our harbour. Very goot German gunfire."* And there we could see our ships nicely sunk in the entrance to the canal, but not by German gunfire. Their funnels were showing above the water and the dredger also nicely sunk. We were taken to the aeroplane shed inside which were six huge planes. On the right were some large concrete buildings which were bomb proof. We were put in one of these and two sentries came in with us with loaded rifles and fixed bayonets. Inside were some wooden beds and we lay down. We had not been there long before there was much shouting and rushing about and we learned that our planes were overhead and the Germans making for cover. Some of the Germans came into the shelter and pushed past our guard. They were looking very angry and one carried one of our entrenching helves weighted at one end with lead and on the other end a piece of string for attaching it to one's wrist and used as a stunning mallet. The Germans knew this, and they were about to bash our brains in with it while our guards looked on, when the situation was saved by the appearance of two officers, who by a few sharp orders, cleared them all out. The officers complimented us on our brave work and being asked if they could give us a hot drink, they sent one man off to get some hot coffee without milk or sugar, but it warmed us up and we felt much better. In return for this kindness I offered to go and undetonate (sic) the Mills grenades which were lying about the mole. I was thinking that some idiot may pick one up when examining it, go off to another world and no doubt they would think we had left them there as traps. The officer, however, declined my offer for he said *"We understand your English bombs."*

At 9am that morning we were taken out and lined up against a wall. The guard loaded their rifles in front of us and we thought at that moment they were going to murder us. Watching us as we stood there were hundreds of soldiers and Belgian workmen, who must have been on the mole that night. A huge camera was brought to the front and we felt safe once more. A photograph was taken of us which was put in the German newspapers. The London Daily Mail copied this photograph and that was the first intimation that our friends had, five weeks later, that we were alive and well. We were now marched off towards Zeebrugge and soon got to where the bridge had been. There was a gap 30 yards long, the girder and railway lines on either side were twisted up like wire. Not a bit of the original bridge was to be seen anywhere; it was just as though someone had lifted it up and carried it off. Two wires had been thrown across the gap and planks were put down on them. We waited until it was finished and then had the order to go across. Whilst I was waiting my turn, a German Captain came to me and after complimenting us on the raid, asked if I had been on active service before. *"Six years"* I replied *"I served through the Cameroons expedition."* *"Well"* he replied *"I am sorry you are captured now for we know you had a hard time out there."* As we went across the temporary bridge one at a time it swayed from side to side. There was a strong tide running underneath, but a motorboat going at full speed against the tide stood by us up should we fall.

We approached the town and could see the effects of the explosion. Windows and doors were blown in and bricks and mortar were lying all over the place. There was not a window anywhere that was not broken. We were taken to a big building and told to wait outside. Smart German officers wearing Iron Crosses came and asked questions, some smiling and some scowling, and quite a number seemed to carry cameras. Inside the building we met an Engine Room Artificer and a stoker both of them from the destroyer North Star. It appears that the destroyer was making for the mole after *Vindictive* had left, perhaps to pick up survivors. The Germans, by a lucky hit, struck her engines and stopped her. Part of the crew got away, with the exception of five men who were accidentally left behind. Two of these were wounded. These five got into a Carley Float and made out to sea. They were well away from land and likely to escape when two German aeroplanes came over, swooped down on them and fired their machine guns killing one and wounding another. The poor fellows jumped into the water and swam about to save themselves being murdered and when the planes moved off again, they regained their float, which is nothing more than a life buoy with a net at the bottom. Two out of the five were alright so they got the Carley Float out to a buoy and tied her up until a German destroyer, which was sent out to them, came along and picked them up. The Germans next morning, seeing the North Star floating helplessly on the waves, turned the battery of 5" guns on her and put her to the bottom. She was a recently built destroyer and no doubt would have been useful to the enemy.

We waited some time in this building waiting to go inside the general office, no doubt to be questioned. German soldiers came and begged our ornaments as curios, but the men did not feel inclined to give them away. We still remembered our comrades on the *Vindictive* and could not favour these men who had not the stomach to come out of their dugouts and put up a fight. One had been a jeweller in London and asked if we had any brilliants or rings to sell and he would give a good price for them. By this time we were getting very hungry and we asked a German if we could soon have something to eat. *"Yah, yah"* he replied *"you want Arbeit?"* That was enough for us to know that the German for food was 'arbeit', so we continued to ask for it. At least one German officer said *"Yah plenty of arbeit in Germany. Cumzee here"* and marched us off to a truck load of timber which we unloaded on to a hand wagon and dragged it round the town for boarding the windows. On asking one of our guards what was the meaning in English of the German word 'arbeit' he replied "Arbeit means work".

Whilst we were out working our planes came over and started bombing. They were flying low and I often wondered if they saw us as we must have been conspicuous in our khaki and steel helmets. In addition we waved to them to attract their notice despite the scowls of our guards who threatened us. The Kaiser came down to Zeebrugge that day but we did not have a very good view of him. He interviewed Captain Palmer and asked him questions about the raid. The Kaiser, after complimenting him on the pluck shown by all ranks, gave orders that the men who were captured were to be treated as heroes all the time they were in Germany. He now offered to shake hands with Captain Palmer, who stood rigidly to attention and refused the proffered hand. It was a beautiful car that the Kaiser travelled in and the cars that accompanied him had machine guns mounted at the back.

We were now taken into the basement of a building and given something to eat. The tables and floor were dirty and rusty knives and forks put down for our use. We had our first taste of black bread and some meat quite black in colour which we understand was horseflesh. Hungry as we were, we could not eat it and the Germans looked rather surprised when we went without. No sooner had we left the table we had a surprise for they went straight to the table to eat it up and from that moment we believed what the British press said about them starving. I for one after this, was prepared to have a rough time in Germany. We asked for a wash, our faces and hands being covered with dirt. A tub was brought along with very hot water and a piece of old sheeting was torn up and handed round. One German brought a very small piece of soap and thinking he was giving it to us, we put our hands out for it. *"One and sixpence"* he said, so we learnt another thing that was scarce in Germany. Some coconut fat was given us and after a good rubbing, we got a little cleaner.

Three Royal Marines including Gunner J W Palmer, Royal Marine Artillery, (RMA 14701) who all took part in the raid of Zeebrugge, 23rd April 1918. © Trustees of the National Museum of the Royal Navy

We were next taken to a building and into some top rooms where we were served out some paper mattresses and told to fill them with shavings. I asked a German Sergeant for some blankets and he said, "You are not allowed blankets, but if you give me tour armaments, I will lend you mine for the night." I refused. About 6pm a German Sergeant and four privates ordered us to fall in outside where the Captain, who we had not seen since our capture, was waiting outside. We were formed up and marched off by a circular route to the canal to go by steamboat to Bruges. I think it would have been more wise on their part had they conducted us there in the darkness for soldiers are always trained to notice everything as they walk about. I noticed on my way the position of guns, searchlights, barbed wire entanglements and trenches at

Zeebrugge. On embarking on the steamboat and going up the canal to Bruges, a distance of 10 miles, I counted 100 ammunition dumps on the left bank and could see they had recently been used. At Bruges docks I noted bomb proof concrete shelters for building submarines, which a German told me later were brought overland in sections and put together at Bruges. German destroyers and submarines were also tied up in the canal and also two small English ships captured by the Germans.

The 12 Royal Marines accidently left behind, photographed soon after their capture. Of them Captain J M Palmer was awarded a bar to the DSC and Sgt H Wright and W H Taylor were awarded the DSM for their services in covering the withdrawal to *HMS Vindictive* whilst on the mole.

On leaving the steamboat we were followed by crowds of Germans and Belgians, the latter seemed to be in sympathy with us. The news spread as we reached the town and whole crowds of Belgians, men, women and children lined up to see us go through. Handkerchiefs were waved to us from windows and tramcars, and such words as 'Well Done England' and 'Brave British Heroes' could be heard on every side. That above all seemed to repay us for our work on the mole. We were marched to a building called the Belfry, a fine building with a high clock tower. We were locked in a room with boarded windows and a sentry put guard over the door. Paper beds and two blankets were served out and we lay down for the night.

Bruges

We turned out next morning at 6.30am and were taken to the courtyard four at a time to have a wash under the pump. We paid the usual 1/6d for a small piece of soap and took one of our blankets down to wipe our faces on. When all had washed two men were sent down for breakfast which consisted of a lump of black bread with the minutest morsel of margarine and tins of black coffee, which to give its proper name was 'burnt barley'. By this time we were hungry enough to eat the bread or part of it. It certainly did taste vile after eating white bread in England and as one man remarked, one had to take a pace forward to swallow it.

We soon learnt that this building was nothing more than a spy centre and the intelligence staff were quartered there. That day we were sent for separately to a cosy consulting room where a German officer of high rank, after asking you to sit down in a nicely padded armchair and to help yourself to cigars or cigarettes, started complimenting you on the brave deed of the British Navy. He then drifted into conversation working gradually to service matters, until the following questions were put to me.

"A Belgian spy is known to have piloted the *Vindictive* through the minefields. Do you know his name?

What was the officer's name who was in charge of this operation?

Did you volunteer for this, if so why?

What kind of food are you having on board ship?

Is it true your sailors are not fitted with gas masks and steel helmets?

What was your idea of landing on the mole?

You belong to the 4th Battalion Royal Marines. Where are the 1st, 2nd and 3rd Battalions and are there any more?

If you are Marines why are you in khaki as all Marines wear blue clothing?

What is your opinion of Lloyd George?

What do the British people think of the war? Are they getting tired of it?"

I would not prove my ignorance by saying I did not know and answered most of the questions by repeatedly remarking *"I cannot tell you"* "Lloyd George" I answered *"was the finest man living and the Britishers loved him and were confident he would bring us successfully through this terrible struggle."* "Yes" he replied *"and we hate him. The war would be finished long before this if he was out of the way."*

"The British people are not tired of the war" I remarked, *"Oh"* he said "then read this letter". He handed me a recently written letter which had been taken off one of my men. This is what I read:

"Oh I do wish this terrible war would end one way or another for I am sick of it and I do hope you will come safely back, etc. etc."

He persisted in asking me about the three battalions to which I replied *"that I did not know there was such battalions and that 4th Battalion was given to us just for the sake of a number"* "But" he said *"we know for certain that the 1st and 2nd Battalions are in France, but it's the 3rd Battalion we want to know about"*

I could have answered that question, but of course I did not. There was not an opening for passing on the information given to us by Captain Carpenter, so I waited another opportunity. I was told I could go and that was the last time I was interviewed, although several of the men had to go before him quite a number of times whilst at Bruges.

Three Belgian ladies came to the Belfry during the forenoon and were given permission to see us. They spoke quite good English and said they belonged to the Belgium Relief Committee. One said she had lived nearly all her life at Coventry but since the war her father had taken seriously ill and cabled her to come. Her father had since got well again but the Germans had refused to let her go back again to England. She conversed in German to our guards and was quite nice to them, but as soon as their backs were turned she shook her fist and said in a whisper *"You wretches. We hate them. Boys be careful what you say to them, they are brutes."* She continued *"The Belgians in Bruges are very happy today, they think your deed very plucky and sent us to find out what they can do for you to repay you for being such great heroes. Are you in need of anything?"* On being told that we had only things we stood up in they replied *"We will bring you something this afternoon."*

In the afternoon they came again and gave each man the following articles: Towels, soap, socks, shirts, caps, handkerchiefs, playing cards, drawers, white bread, compressed meat and cakes, but the greatest surprise of all was, after serving us out with English cigarettes, they handed each man a roll of notes, with 20 marks in each roll and equal to about £1 in English money. They came several times to see us bringing something to eat and English cigarettes. We gave them our ornaments and steel helmets as curios, and when they came the next time they were wearing the ornaments as brooches having had them gilted over and pins put on them. These young ladies had brothers fighting in the Belgian Army but although they had been fighting for over four years, the girls had never heard from them; and only in the case of death did they get any news. They were allowed only one hour to converse with us and as a rule a German who could speak English came in with them. Each lady had a passport with her photograph on it which they had to show whenever demanded.

Thirteen Belgians had been arrested for spying in connection with the Zeebrugge raid and some of them were finally found guilty and shot. Belgian girls were employed in the buildings doing all kinds of work, some tidying up the courtyard and others labouring. One day, whilst having a wash, a young girl was pumping water into a bucket. It was hard work, for the pump was a heavy one. A big German soldier came up to the pump, lifted her bucket off and putting his own on stood with his hands on his hips whilst she commenced to fill it. Just then a marine went to the pump, took the handle off the girl and filled the bully's bucket. He got for his pains a sweet smile from the girl and a scowl from the bully.

Our daily diet at this place was, in the morning black bread and coffee, at 12 noon soup, and some more soup at 6pm, but as this stuff was too vile to eat our German guards would eat it for us. During the evenings we were allowed out in the passage for about two hours to take exercise. As we strolled up and down we would sing all the latest English songs and the German soldiers would gather round to hear us, some asking for Tipperary and we would sing it for them. One day whilst in the room we sang the Marseillaise and were singing quite heartily when some Belgians walking in the street stopped to listen and started laughing. We could look out onto the main street through cracks in the boards. We were ordered after this not to sing the Marseillaise.

A German marine came in one evening for a chat. He said he had been a valet at the C……. Hotel in London. He knew London quite well and said the manager was still corresponding with him through a friend in Switzerland. He said he was very well known in London for all the gentry knew 'Big Fritz'. He was delighted when I told him that I had last Monday's *Daily Sketch* in my pocket and I gave it to him to read in exchange for a cigar. He wanted to know the price of whisky and tobacco which seemed to interest him.

Having seen some Goth China exhibited in a shop window across the road, I asked a German to get me it, but on explaining to the Belgian shopkeeper that it was for a prisoner captured on the mole, he sent me a beautiful piece and would not accept any money for it. I carried that bit of china hundreds of miles across Belgium and Germany and finally got it home without breaking it.

A young German of the intelligence staff would come in during the evenings to have a chat with us and what he said, to improve his English. We asked his version about the Nurse Cavell affair. *"The Germans were quite in the right of course"* he said, but on the other hand he continued *"We done wrong in shooting her and also sinking the Lusitania because your English papers cried out so much about it, that we now have the whole world against us. You forget the French are shooting our women spies, and they shot a woman before we did."* He was a young fellow of about 25 and if he expected any information of any value he was greatly mistaken. We certainly filled him with a lot of nonsense, most of which he took in. His opinion of the war was that either side could win and that it would last for years. When I told him I was confident that we would be the winners before Christmas 1918, he burst into hearty laughter. *"That is impossible,"* he remarked.

The German band played in the square each day from 12 to 1pm, some of the tunes one had often heard played in England since the war. One day we had the pleasure of seeing Admiral Sheer reviewing some thousands of German marines and sailors after which was played the National Anthem which was similar to ours. At the finish they marched past doing the famous goose step.

English books were sent in by the Belgians and we were also given three cards to fill in to be sent back to England. We were informed that these cards, notifying our friends that we were prisoners of war would reach England via Holland in four days. As a matter of fact they took exactly six weeks.

After one week in the Belfry the German officer of the Intelligence Staff came in looking not very pleased. He had in his hand a well-known London paper. He asked *"what we meant by unfair fighting on the mole. If it was true that we clubbed their men, bit them, stabbed them, and even used our fists,"* He also said there was a report going round that we hooked the eyes out of their wounded. We had been served out with new knives prior to leaving England and like all soldiers' knives there was a spike on it. Our Captain was not there, so being the senior I tried to explain the case to him, telling him *"the spikes were not for that purpose, and also that the Germans would not come out and fight us on the mole, and that we saw very few of them before we were captured,"* He replied *"You are a liar Sergeant. Read this English paper."* There in the columns of a well-known London paper was all the rot that a press representative could think of. How we dashed the mole, bayonetted, spiked, clubbed and bit the enemy and the fighting was so fierce that we even got to using our fists. There was certainly nothing about killing the wounded or hooking their eyes out. *"Your English papers never tell lies"* he said *"so you will hear more of this"* Our comments on the English papers were, I am afraid, not very complimentary and had the reporter been there he would have had a pretty rough time of it.

The convict prison was a huge building with very long corridors and rows of cells three storeys high on either side. Men were undergoing sentences for murder, spying, etc, but the majority we learnt afterwards, were sailors serving 15 years and life sentences for refusing to go to sea in submarines. One German soldier in the cell near us was serving a 15 year sentence for brutally murdering a Belgian farmer and robbing him. The cell we occupied was partitioned off by glass and in this little recess was a filthy heap of mattresses, which were to be our beds, and four iron buckets were in the cell for our uses. Another bucket with some water for us to wash in, one table and two chairs were the only furniture. With 12 of us in this cell there was hardly room for us to move about, but we made the most of it and settled down as best we could. There were bars of iron over the windows and the door made of steel and oak was six inches thick.

We were served out with a bowl, spoon and towel, and that night we were served with bean soup. The warder coming down the passage with a huge bunch of keys would unlock the massive door and shout something in German and we would go outside and get into single file. As we went past a ladle of soup would be given to us. The warders stood and grinned as we lined up, and shouted and sneered at us as we went inside. Next day we had coffee in the morning for breakfast with nothing to eat; 12 noon bean soup (horse beans) for dinner; black bread and margarine for tea; and that was our daily ration. By this time we were hungry enough to eat their food and would look forward to meal times.

During the afternoon we were taken down to a little enclosure, triangular in shape, with a little garden in the centre. On either side of us was a 20 foot high wall. They must have thought us dangerous criminals, for in addition to being locked in this enclosure, there was a German Warder with a loaded revolver set to watch us. Had we thought of escaping they did not give us much time for we were only allowed half an hour exercise each day. Some of our German warders could speak English and they used it to mean advantage, for many a caustic remark we heard about our beloved country, and Britannia ruling the waves and about us trying to starve Germany. We choked back our hasty replies. No doubt a word to these bullies would have meant a bayonet thrust in our bodies, and of course a charge of mutiny brought against us.

Sometimes they would not allow us to empty our buckets with the result that they would overflow in the cell and we would live in the most disgusting conditions. We would also get very thirsty after drinking some extra salty soup and only those who have been locked in a stinking enclosure with a burning thirst know the agony we suffered. We got so thirsty one night that we hammered the door for over an hour until a warder came to see what was wrong but on being told he slammed the door with the words *"English swine"*. The water tap was only a short distance up the passage. Our life became quite unbearable under these circumstances, so the men proposed that I should see the Governor of the prison.

The day when we were taken out for exercise I passed a warder who I knew could speak English quite well. I halted in front of him, and looking him square in the face I said to him *"I wish to see the Governor of the prison and if I don't see him today, I will stop him at the first opportunity and report you for not telling him."* I had the pleasure now of seeing the bully turn to coward; his face went white as he asked me *"Can I do anything for you?" "No"* I replied *"You can't; I am determined to see the Governor."* I now re-joined the others for my exercise. We had not been back to our cell long before my name was called out and I was escorted to the Governor's office. It is not often one sees a German officer with a kind face, but let me say here that this man had one. Turning to my escort of warders he curtly ordered them out of the office and said to me *"Well Sergeant, what can I do for you?" "Sir"* I replied *"We are honourable prisoners of war and it is not the usual thing in England to put prisoners of war in common criminal establishments herded together in a cell. May I ask that we be sent from here as soon as possible."* He replied *"I am sorry for you; we know it is not the usual thing but it is not my fault. Officers in higher authority put you here. I will send a report to the Commandant. Is* that all you want Sergeant?" "No, sir" I replied *"We are disciplined troops and of course we don't wish to give any trouble, but why should your warders sneer and laugh at us every turn and pass insulting remarks about the country we belong to. Is it your wish that we should not be allowed to empty our buckets so that they run over in the cell? Cannot we have water when we are almost dying of thirst and have a little more exercise in the afternoon and better food?"*

As I continued his face changed from a smile to sternness. *"Is this true about the warders?"* "Yes" I replied with some heat *"and my comrades will bear witness if you wish."* "Leave this matter to me Sergeant. I am glad you reported it and you will be treated much better in the future. You can have two hours exercise in the afternoon, a bath once a week, water when you want it, and for a warder to answer your door when you knock. You can also request to see me whenever you like, but mind you I don't want any frivolous complaints. Of course as regards better food, I cannot alter that for I don't get much better food than you are getting, but I will send the Belgian nuns to see you and perhaps they will bring you food." After thanking him I was taken back to the cell and I informed the others of everything that was said.

Things now got much better. The warders treated us with the greatest respect for they seemed to dread the Governor. If they did anything wrong they were punished by being relieved of their job and sent to the front; and this seemed to have a bigger hold on them than anything else. As I did not complain again, the Governor came round to the cell and asked if we were being treated better and we replied *"Yes"*. I asked permission to buy cigarettes outside and smoke in the cell. He at once turned to the warder and ordered him to buy things for us when we wished. These warders, when being spoken to, would stand to attention with a click of the heels, salute, and sometimes tremble and I saw very few of them who could look their superiors straight in the face. The officers had a way of speaking to them as if they were dogs and very often finish a sentence in a loud and commanding voice which sounded like a clap of thunder. I never, in my service career, have seen discipline carried to such a pitch and I don't know that I would care to see it in the British Army. If a German officer was walking down one of the corridors, the warders would hide out of sight although you would see plenty of them as soon as he had gone.

The governor kept his promise and the nuns came in next day to see us. They were two old ladies and I shall always remember their faces as they came into our stinking cell and saw the filthy mattresses used as beds. They simply put their hands up over their heads and said *"Oh"* which spoke volumes. They could not speak English but turning to the Governor they said quite a lot in German. I am not of Roman Catholic faith myself but I shall always speak well of them in the future. These good souls brought us in good wholesome food every day comprising white bread, potatoes, sometimes peas and turnips and, about once a week some fat bacon. They went round the town and collected cigars, tobacco and cigarettes for us and supplied us with mending material and English books; and they did everything in their power to make our lives a little happier. Each week they took our dirty washing and bought it back beautifully clean and mended. We all had photographs of our dear ones at home and the nuns were greatly interested in these and they could see by the photos the kind of homes to which we belonged. Some of our lads were married and on being shown a photo of three beautiful children belonging to Sergeant Taylor, tears came into their eyes.

I think the life would have driven us mad in that cell had it not been for the 'Bing Boys' as we called our airmen who without fail, came over every night to bomb Bruges docks which were only a short distance away. At 12 midnight the fun would always start. Bruges was swarming with anti-aircraft guns most of which seemed to be stationed just round the prison. The performance was opened by the whirring noise of the propellers, then a succession of green lights would be fired into the air in the direction of the planes. Very powerful searchlights would now be turned on and would very quickly find the planes. There were our lads riding as it were, on the top of the beam of light so slow it seemed to us that we could almost see the men themselves. Bravery – why I think it even put our stint in the shade. We had a good view of them as they came gently along in their proper formation, and then the barrage would start such a deafening noise that it would almost break our eardrums. Pieces of shrapnel and shell would fall all around the prison. Shells would be bursting under, over, right and left of the machines, but undaunted our brave airmen came on, and then a deafening roar as the bombs began to fall, which seemed to shake the earth. They may have dropped one on the prison by accident, but we did not think of that. Whoever took part in those raids have the heartiest thanks of the 12 marines locked in that reeking cell. All the time we were there we only heard of one machine being brought down and of only one bomb being dropped in the town by mistake. Daytime they would also come over, but we did not derive so much sport then as we did at night time, as they were too high up.

The Governor gave us permission to write letters to England and as many as we liked. A few of these letters finally reached England but the address at the top was always inked over so that a reply could not be sent. I wrote to Admiral Keyes on behalf of the men, but of course mentioning nothing detrimental to the Germans. We were told that we would get replies in a week or two, but we little thought then that it would be six months before we got our first news from home. Even this dull existence had its amusing side. One evening a piece of rolled rag with a string attached to it was lowered down in front of our bars from the cell above. There was a note inside with a silver half mark and the note, on being opened, we found the following message. *'We have no cigarettes, mister. Will you put some in for us. Thank you mister. From an old sailor.'* Of course we sent some up for him and bought more with the money. The other prisoners corresponded with each other in the same manner from window to window. It was rather amusing to watch one prisoner trying to swing a message from one window to another on a level with him. The bars were small and the window misty glass so that he could not see the string or message, neither could the other man; but they were directed by other prisoners from their cells who could see both windows and shouted directions. The struggle lasted over an hour and caused much amusement.

One day a warder watching us while out airing saw the prisoners swinging messages and smilingly remarked *"Very Good"* and took notice of the cell. One of the cells in the top storey overlooked the high wall and outside of the prison. Each night at dusk the man in this cell would swing his line over the wall and his friends outside the prison would send him up food and messages. The convicts had no work to do in the prison with the exception of keeping their cells clean. They were allowed half an hour exercise each day. From our cell window overlooking one of the little compounds we saw four Belgians out for an airing. One of them was a priest and could speak English and the German guarding them allowed us to converse. He told us he was a spy and had done a lot of good work for England but the enemy had not been able to get enough to shoot him so he was given 15 years penal servitude. With him was an old man, a retired Belgian officer who had been sentenced to death for spying and then at the last minute the sentence of death had been commuted to one of penal servitude for life in close confinement. The old man seemed to be broken hearted and would not last long. We told him about our raid and the news about the Americans landing in France and what was taking place on the Western Front making things as bright as possible in the short time we had and also gave them tobacco. Some warders coming down unexpectedly saw us giving them the tobacco and marched them in and we never saw them anymore. Before going, the priest gave us the blessing but I don't know who needed it most, himself or us.

Early one morning at 3.30am, a German came into our cell and said he wanted three men, so the other Sergeant and two men left us to have a bath as we thought then, but as they did not come back we concluded they had gone to Germany. It was no good asking the warders for they said *"I don't know"* to everything we asked. We had been just one month in the cell when one day a German came along and after taking our names said *"I think you will be going to Germany either today or tomorrow"*, but in half an hour's time he came back and informed us that we had got to go now and told us to pack our gear and fall in outside which we quickly did. Seeing the Governor outside I thanked him for doing what he could for us and he replied *"that he would go and see the nuns and tell them we were going and they would bring us some food."* In a short time he returned with them and each man was served with bread and cigarettes. We were marched all round the back streets so that the people could not see us and finally arrived at the station where we had to wait nearly an hour for a train.

While waiting for the train we saw a little Belgian boy between two burly Germans and the boy sobbing as though his heart would break. By this time some Belgian soldiers, also under escort, arrived on the station and were to travel with us. We could see, by the broken glass and holes in the roof, that it had been well bombed by our airmen. The train arrived at last but I could not understand how an engine like that could go along. Every particle of it was rusty with the rust having eaten away parts of the steel. The carriages however were not so bad as foreign carriages go. We got eight men in a carriage with the German sentries.

There was an air raid in progress as we left the town. The train was a slow one and passed through some very flat country. Every bit of ground seemed to be under cultivation with the chief products being rye, potatoes and a few fields of wheat. In quite a number of fields were Belgian women and girls kneeling in a row weeding. It was a beautiful day and after being penned up in the prison for a month, we quite enjoyed the journey.

On arriving at Ghent we had to change and got on an express. Over 4,000 German soldiers, evidently bound for the front were just entraining. These troops were well kitted up, well clothed and were looking remarkably fit and well, each man carrying an extra pair of boots and a good thick rug. Whatever may be the condition of the German people, their soldiers are certainly well fed, but how miserable they looked; not a smile on any of their faces and they looked at us as if to say *"You lucky fellows to be prisoners"*, although at that moment I wished I was anywhere else but in their clutches. After waiting for the train to fill up we were allotted two special carriages. Our sentries now told us we were not going to Germany but to a concentration camp at Cortrai.

On getting off the train we were marched through the streets to a camp occupied by the French, and as we waited for admittance, we saw the French soldiers all lined up to draw their evening meal. They smiled and nodded to us. After waiting a considerable time outside we were now informed that it would be dangerous to put us in with the French for they were embittered against us because of our great retirement on the Western Front, and, said one of our escort, they would knife us if we were put with them. We were now marched back through the town and whilst waiting at a level crossing for a train load of Belgian workers to pass, they gave us three hearty cheers. We would have responded had not our escort checked us in time.

Cortrai

We finally got to the concentration camp which was a large building and had been a police station in pre-war times. There were 24 small rooms. At the back of the building was a courtyard 15 yards long by 10 yards wide with buildings all round it occupied by German soldiers. In the courtyard were about 30 Frenchmen, 40 Belgians and 50 Englishmen belonging to different regiments, and also our three comrades who had preceded us from Bruges. We were given some black bread and butter and taken across to a stable to sleep. On the floor was some straw and we were given a blanket each. The place was infested with rats and we did not sleep very well that night. We got the same diet the next day as we did at Bruges, coffee in the morning, soup at dinner and bread for tea.

During the day we were sent for individually and had to give the following details – name, regiment, battalion, married or single, address in England, and where captured. We were then marched off to a building a quarter of a mile away and told to strip and hand in our clothes to be fumigated. In the meantime we had a shower bath and when our clothes were finished, we dressed and were marched back. We were next told off for rooms. The one I occupied with three others had three dirty mattresses and a few blankets. The floor was in a filthy condition not having been washed for years. All over the walls were written the names and addresses of hundreds of our boys who had been captured in Belgium. The door was made of very strong wood with a pigeon hole in it. It was locked every night at 10 pm. The soup at this place was fairly good and a quarter of a loaf a day was enough to live on despite the fact that we were always hungry. During the day we went to physical exercises; sometimes I would take the men, sometimes the other Sergeant. It was quite voluntary but we always had a large attendance. After this we would take part in games and enjoy ourselves as best we could, for whatever the conditions one very rarely sees Englishmen very unhappy.

One thing that struck me as rather peculiar at Cortrai was that there were quite a number of German NCOs who could speak English quite well. These men intermixed with the English freely and discussed the war and politics. I think most of us knew they were out to get information from us and most of the lads fought shy of them. Most of the German NCOs had been in England before the war in good business positions. I often got into conversation with them and it was surprising the information they would always give away, although I was careful not to give any myself. Speaking one day to a German Sergeant the conversation drifted to signalling, he having asked me the meaning of the crossed flags I was wearing. He asked me quite unexpectedly if I understood anything about the Fullerphone, and on my replying in the negative he started, much to my surprise, to tell me all about it. He said that the Germans knew for certain that the English had no faith in the instrument and the Germans could detect messages just the same. On my asking him to explain how, he seemed to fight shy of answering. *"Your signallers"* he continued *"are very careless for when they are captured all kinds of important documents are found on them, things that the Germans very much want to know. Your code messages are also very easily deciphered,"* he said. *"That is impossible,"* I replied, but he explained to me that if a key word was two or three days old it would easily slip across to the German lines. *"Plenty of good information,"* he said, *"was obtained by signallers getting into conversation with one another. I know it is not allowed by your officers,"* he continued, *"but for all that, it does happen. Such things as this. 'Is Private Jones there of the 2nd Yorks?', letting us know that the Yorkshire Regiment was in a certain sector."* He also explained to me that during the recent withdrawal, signals were being sent to the effect that the Germans were surrounding our troops and S.O.S. signals for assistance. *"These signals,"* he said, *"were picked up by the Germans and sent on at once by wireless to Berlin in an amazing short time, for it was not necessary for the German staff to make reports when the British were doing it for them. This also,"* he continued, *"was a good guide for the Germans not to send troops where they were not wanted."* He told me there was a big staff of German NCOs working behind the German lines whose duty it was to do nothing else but tap messages and get information.

Our conversation now drifted to organisation and he went on to say that there were two men in charge of our great armies on the Western Front alone, each of them working separately and with a certain amount of enmity. Hindenburg, he continued, was in charge of the whole German Army all over the world, and whatever was happening on either front, Hindenburg must know all about it and sanction it. All important messages on the Western Front sent to the various

British prisoners lying by the roadside having been allowed a short rest

commanders were despatched by motor car or motor cyclist, a big staff of German officers being kept for that purpose. *"We rely very little on signalling and wireless,"* little on he said. *"Letters found on prisoners were of vast importance. Your English Tommie liked to keep his love letters and of course we get them when he is captured. These letters tell us a very important thing ie, the opinion of the British public regarding the war, what the food situation is like, and even the state of the weather, especially if the letter came from a farm. A farmer will also talk of his crops, just the thing we want to know. We have a big staff of experts who translate the English letters into German and pick out information, and then the letters are burnt."*

Blockships used during the raid on Zeebrugge, Belgium, 1918. In the background is the Mole on which the 4th Battalion landed

All this information was given to me quite voluntarily by a German Sergeant who until recently, had been employed since the commencement of hostilities behind the German lines doing nothing else but getting information. He was wearing the Iron Cross and other decorations for doing this special work.

There was a canteen in the camp which was run by a German Jew, The articles bought in this canteen were just double the price of what one would pay in town. There are a large number of Jews in the German army and run nearly all the canteens, some of which are near the firing line. Under the archway was a huge map and during the great German advance the sectors of ground they had taken were marked off every day. The German NCOs were in good spirits and the one who had given me so much information came up to me, tapped me on the back and said *"Well Sergeant, we shall be the winners now by Christmas 1918 not the English I'm thinking. Have you seen the map this morning? Why we shall be in Paris in less than a week." "Perhaps so"* I remarked, and turned away.

Great slices of ground were marked off every day until 3rd June, and then from 3rd to 7th June nothing was put on the board. The Germans were walking about with long faces and if one dared to ask how the war was progressing, one would get an angry reply. One or two recently captured prisoners arrived in camp and said the Germans were being driven back with heavy losses and likely to be cut off altogether so our spirits rose and the Germans' fell.

After being at the camp for some time we were given a letter card to write home and were informed that it would take four weeks to reach England. This card folded into four pieces and we could write quite a lot on it. About once every eight days some of us were allowed out for a walk. A German Sergeant who could speak English and two sentries with loaded rifles accompanied us. We were taken through the town into the country and along the banks of a river where the sentries, two old men, soon got tired, and much against our will we had to sit down on the grass. On either side of the river were fields of flax which had been cut and stacked like corn. Some of it was put through a certain process by soaking in the river and weighed down with stones.

After a rest we would have games, racing, wrestling or anything else to pass the time. The German NCO would give cigars or cigarettes as prizes. For the 100 yards race we had to go up the field and run back. There was plenty of undergrowth and as we walked up the field I thought what a good opportunity to escape. Both the sentries had the barrels of their rifles corroded for I had noticed that, in addition to them being old men, anyone trying to escape would have a good 100 yards start, but they didn't trust us and one of the sentries hobbled up the field with us. We now turned for home after being away for over two hours. The Belgians en route would give us things to eat, but it was strictly forbidden, notices being put up in camp saying that if any man is caught receiving anything he will be severely punished, and also the people of the town. This of course is done to avoid the risk of passing messages.

The Germans were very angry about articles in the London Times dealing with the ill-treatment of prisoners in German prison camps. Talking to a German one day on the subject, he asked me if I thought the Germans ill-treated their prisoners. *"I do"* I replied heatedly, and instantly asked him if being cast in prison with common criminals, 12 men in one cell for a month, was proper treatment for an honourable prisoner of war. *"Oh yes"* he replied, *"I acknowledge that was not right."* He next brought up the subject of ill-treatment of German prisoners in the Colonies and said they were being treated worse than the natives. I replied that I served in an expedition in one of their colonies, but saw no ill-treatment in any of them, and when we were bringing them home to England they were given the best parts of the ship to live in whilst we occupied the worst.

One day I was asked by a German officer if I would like to go for a walk with him the following morning about 7.30am. He said *"I shall not be armed and you will accompany me as a friend, but you must give your word of honour not to escape."* I accepted, so at 7.30 I was ready under the archway when I found there were two of them and not one. I was taken all around the town, shown places of interest and was given a very good time. Cigars and cigarettes were given to me and it being beautiful day I enjoyed myself very much. Belgian women were working in the roads, and seeing a lot of old women lined up I asked the reason and was informed that they were very poor people and had food given to them free every day by the nuns. I was shown around the park and watched a large body of troops on their way to the front. A certain sector, the officer explained to me, was getting weak and those were the reinforcements. Belgian ladies handed me cigars as I passed and the officers looked the other way so that I could accept them. They did most of the talking and asked quite a lot of questions about naval affairs, but of course, I would not tell them. I knew I was being given a good outing for something and was wondering what it was when one of the Germans pointed to a Red Cross ambulance and I was told that it was the only vehicle allowed to use rubber, all other cars and cycles had springs round their wheels. I was informed that Germany got all their rubber from the Cameroons and as she had lost that colony they now had no rubber. Having brought up the subject of the Cameroons I was told that colony was of vital importance to them.

They now informed me that they had read an article in the German papers that a Sergeant captured on the Mole had served in the Cameroons and it would be a good opportunity to get an Englishman's version of that expedition as I was the only prisoner who had served out there. It appears that the German officer I had spoken to on the Mole had reported that I was there. This information was put to me very nicely but I said nothing.

That evening after getting back I was surprised to be sent for by my German companions and asked into the consulting room. On the table was a large map of the Cameroons and also an article supposed to have been written by an English Sergeant Major who had served in East Africa. I was now asked if I would write an article dealing with the conduct of the German troops in West Africa, what became of the stocks of rubber in the country at the commencement of the war, what I knew about the white ant pest and if the plantations, especially the rubber, were still under cultivation. Of course I flatly refused to do any such thing. *"But why should you not write it?"* he said *"The expedition is finished and here is a report written by an Englishman on the East African campaign. Even Sir Douglas Haig has written articles on the operations on the Western Front, so what harm is there in your writing on a small thing like that?"* *"Because"* I replied *"I may betray my country in so doing; perhaps say something they would not like me to say and as the colonies would, in all probability, play a very important part in the peace conference. I might, in writing, give a missing link in a chain of evidence which the Germans want very badly."* *"You need not say anything about your government"* he replied *"or sign your name to the paper if you do not wish."* *"I shall not write the article"* I said. *"Now look here Sergeant"* he continued *"If you do this we will make your life as pleasant as possible all the time you are in Germany. We will find you a good job if you don't wish to go back to England and we'll take care your country know nothing about it."* *"But I very much want to go back to England"* I replied *"and as soon as possible. I tell you finally I shall not write the article."*

I was now threatened by them and they said there were ways and means of making me write and I should be pestered to death at every camp I went to until I did write it. I said something in return but the officers got in such a temper at being baulked that I thought if I valued my life I must keep my mouth close. *"Can I go now?"* I asked *"Yes you can"* he snarled *"and we will report this to Berlin and you will hear more of it."*

One day I was given the English Times and asked if I would read a certain article to all the Englishmen in the camp. The article dealt with a munitions factory and how our men had been made by cruelty to work in the German factory making munitions against their wish. The Times was dated 29th May 1918 and I read it on 10th June. A German officer who had been employed at the same factory as an overseer was afterwards going to tell us the article was a lot of rot and explain to us the true facts of the case. The men got together to hear what he had to say but he didn't turn up. I went and asked him if he would come and he said *"some day when I am not busy"*. I told him I could get the men together at a minute's notice if he would let me know. We had a nice lot of questions ready for him on the subject and would have enjoyed a good argument. I asked him several times and finally gave it up as a bad job, and believed The Times.

We had three English Flying Officers in camp and one day after an air raid, these officers accompanied by a guard, went out in the town for a walk. The Belgians were quite hostile to them and even went so far as to try and get hold of them, the guards having quite a difficulty in protecting them. It appears that our airmen had the day before been over Cortrai and by accident dropped a bomb on the town killing some women and children.

The Belgian ladies came most days and brought food and other things for the men who needed it. The officers in the camp were well looked after by them and many a dainty feed they got each day. The Belgian soldiers resented this for the Germans allowed an article to appear in the Belgian press asking the people if they knew that the men who were getting the best of the food sent into the camps were the very men who were killing their women and children in the air raids over Cortrai. We loved our officers. They were a jolly lot of fellows mixing with us in our games and giving us food and cigarettes that they could spare. I have mentioned all this to expose the dirty under-handed way the Germans had of trying to breed discontent amongst the various nationalities then quartered in the camp. The Germans spoke well of the marines having organised sports and physical drill amongst the others. They would stand for hours and watch us and pass remarks that were the jolliest crowd they had seen at Cortrai. We had an old piano in one of the rooms and there we would gather in the evenings. We had plenty of men who thought they could sing and we used to enjoy ourselves very much, everyone taking part in the choruses. A song entitled 'Are we downhearted? No' we would sing with much gusto and nearly bring the house down. We were allowed to sing 'God Save The King' and we would sing it very heartily. I must mention here that this was the only camp we were allowed to sing it in.

One of our songs 'haven't seen the Kaiser for a h… of a time' was quickly suppressed by a German coming into the room with a h… of a temper. I was rather surprised one day to see our friend, the Engine Room Artificer, who was captured off the destroyer North Star come into camp dressed in khaki and wearing the rank of Company Sergeant-Major. On arriving at Cortrai from Bruges, he had been given khaki and two crowns and sent off to a camp at Wellfagen to take charge of 300 Englishmen who were working behind the German lines. He was responsible, he told me, that these men turned out at 4.30 am and had to be at work at 5am. They were employed laying rails just in rear of the firing line. For this very dangerous work the privates were paid 2/6d for every 10 days work and NCOs who were forced to take charge of them got 5/- every tenth day. Our aeroplanes often came over and bombed them and seven men one day got severely wounded. Next day they refused to go to work, but were driven there with prods of the bayonet and butt end of the rifle.

On 14th June 10 of us had orders to get our gear outside and at 3pm we marched off to the station to proceed to a place called Inglemunster. We took with us a trolley load of parcels which had just arrived from England and belonged to men working at Inglemunster. These parcels, according to the date, had taken four months to do the journey. On getting to the station we were informed there was no train running to Inglemunster so we had orders to leave the parcels on the platform and bring back the empty trolley. We pointed out to the guard that they might be stolen and asked him to put them into some building or bring them back to camp, but he curtly ordered us to leave them there. I expect those parcels were amongst the many thousands sent from England for the express purpose of helping to feed the German people. We were told we should only have stayed at Inglemunster for the night and then proceeded to Germany the next day.

On arriving back at camp a German officer called the roll and 20 of us fell in on the right. The party comprised 5 marines, 2 Engine Room Artificers, 1 Stoker, 3 Australians and 9 English soldiers. We were told to be ready to leave at 9am the following morning. On falling in the next day we received a third of a loaf of black bread and after many handshakes of our comrades left behind, we marched to the station. Just before leaving a German Sergeant came to me and said quite confidentially that owing to bad treatment we had endured at Bruges we were going to be sent to the best prisoner of war camp in Germany, but the readers can decide for themselves as I proceed with these experiences. On our way to the station we passed 20 of our men just going to work. Their clothes were all greasy and no doubt they were working at some factory in the town. They were not looking very happy and only smiled sadly as we started singing the song 'Good-Bye' as we went marching by.

On arriving at the station we saw some Belgian refugees, about 50 in number, waiting to board the same train as us. They were nearly all young men and had an escort of German soldiers who were marching them off to some place for work. A special coach having been put on the troop train for our special benefit, we got in seven men in a compartment and the Belgian workmen got in behind. Some English and French officers also boarded the train. In each compartment there was a sentry with a loaded revolver on his belt.

The train left and the journey was uneventful with the exception that we saw young Belgian girls felling trees in a large wood and making woodwork for trenches, helping indirectly the Germans to kill their own brothers, but forced to do it. As we got to St Dennis we saw Belgian women doing all kinds of manual labour, for this station was a large railway centre. There was a huge aerodrome. Every particle of ground was under cultivation and the crops remarkably good. Liquid manure which is used extensively in Belgium and Germany was being drawn by oxen and sprinkled on the fields. German soldiers seemed to be drilling everywhere about the country.

Having left Cortrai at 9.45am, we arrived at Ghent at 11am and were taken to a large underground room and locked in. On the walls were written thousands of names of men of all nationalities and where they were captured. There were also a few very uncomplimentary remarks about the Kaiser and his army. This shed had no doubt been used for a long time as a dumping place for prisoners to await trains. At 12 noon we were given some soup and at 4 o'clock we entrained for Dendermonde where we arrived at 5.15pm. On getting out of the station we were told to get into columns of fours, our officers having left us at Ghent and gone in another direction. We marched along a beautiful country road, the Belgians nodding to us as we passed. They would have spoken to us if they had dared but they seemed afraid of our guard.

Dendermonde

The town itself was in ruins with only a few buildings left standing. Almost every house in the place was knocked down by gunfire but the streets were clear of debris and the people had tried to rebuild their houses again by placing bricks one on top of the other without mortar. Quite a number of people were living in these temporary put-up buildings. The population of Dendermonde before the war was 30,000 but a Belgian told me later that only 2,000 people now lived there. One church I noticed was demolished, but another one, although the houses on either side were in ruins, had hardly been touched. It had been hit in only one place and very little damage done to it.

It took us 20 minutes to march from the station to our destination which comprised some large barracks, before the war occupied by Belgian troops. The barracks was built on similar lines to ours in England with the barrack square in the middle for drill purposes and had accommodation for 5,000 troops. The barracks was now used by the Germans for concentrating prisoners of war of all nationalities prior to sending them on their way to Germany. Just before our arrival 2,000 allied prisoners had left for Germany and the barracks was now empty. The 20 men on arrival halted in the square and a German Sergeant called out our names. *"Step out to the front any man who knows anything about ship building."* One man went forward and he took his name and particulars. He next asked for iron workers but no-one else went to the front. We were given papers to fill in similar to the cards we got at Bruges notifying our friends at home that we were prisoners and quite well. As soon as this was done we were taken to a large barrack room where on either side was strewn a lot of shavings and a blanket each. This of course was our beds. We enquired if we could get any food that night as we were all very hungry. *"Oh yes"* said the Sergeant *"you will get a hot supper which is already cooking in the cookhouse"* and we would receive it at 7pm. We felt very thankful and looked forward to our feed, but imagine our surprise and disgust when after lining up and eagerly waiting for some time at the cookhouse, we were finally given a bowl of cabbage water and nothing else. I would not like to put it in print what some of our fellows said on receiving this but it was certainly a big blow to hungry men. To add insult to injury the German soldiers grinned sarcastically at us as we passed them carrying our bowls of cabbage water.

Our daily ration at these barracks were a quarter loaf of black bread and coffee at 8am; a basin of very thin soup at 12 noon; and another basin at 7pm. This soup was some days thickened with a little barley, but most days it was just coloured water. We were rather lucky the first three days for the Belgians sent us some lard, but the Germans took charge of this and when it was served out to us it amounted to the very minutest morsel per man. I am not going to say that we were dying of starvation but speaking personally the terrible gnawing hunger nearly drove me mad. I fell away in weight and got very weak. The black bread I would cut in two and eat one half for breakfast and the other for supper, chewing it over as long as possible before swallowing it.

I saw men at this camp crying for food. Near the WCs was a heap of rubbish comprising cabbage stalks, potato peelings, onion leaves, etc which the Germans had thrown away. Why they did not boil it up with the soup is a mystery to me for it certainly would have made it more nourishing. Our lads went round this corner daily and sorted the heaps over, picking out bits and pieces here and there and eating them.

At 5am on 19th June some 500 British Tommies came into barracks. These men had been collected at various camps in Belgium, and most of them had been captured at the great German offensive of April and May 1918. Some had been put in forts, some in prisons, but the majority had been working behind the German lines. Quite a number of these poor fellows had been wounded by our own shell fire. Our aeroplanes came over and dropped leaflets telling the Germans if our men kept working behind the lines the English and French would make reprisals and do likewise. To describe the condition of these men is not easy, but if you imagine what a party of men look like after carrying coal on their backs from a coal lighter to a battleship and have just finished after 24 hours work, then you know what these men looked like, instead of coal dust imagine dirt. A more dirty or dejected lot of men I have never seen or want to see again. They looked thin and worn out, their clothing in rags. Their boots were worn out and some without boots with their feet bleeding. Some of the fellows, I learnt afterwards, had their good boots taken off them by the Germans and others had sold them to buy food. Their steel helmets, having been taken off them, they were wearing straw hats, top hats and any other kind of head gear and some men even wearing German soldier's hats.

As they marched through the town some of the Belgians had taken their hats off their heads and thrown them to our boys. Some of these men, especially those who had been locked in prison had not seen any soap or water for six weeks. The dirt was actually caked on their bodies, they were covered with vermin and looked downright ill. On being told the kind of food we were getting, they confessed they had been having the same for six weeks. They had sold all their belongings to get food, such as rings given them in many cases by some loving mother, wife or sweetheart, watches, etc. When these poor fellows were dismissed, quite a number of them went round to the rubbish heaps and there was very little left a short time afterwards.

The German sentries stood and grinned at our starving comrades, and yet today when the war is over, one reads how Germany is starving and how England and America are doing their utmost to get food to them. Let me tell my readers (and most prisoners won't tell you) that no-one in the world has suffered the pangs of hunger as a British prisoner of war and very few Germans at this present moment know what hunger is as we knew it. I am not vindictive (although I belong to that ship) and if the Germans had done anything to help these poor fellows I would have mentioned it here. That night they got their usual cabbage water soup, not much of a feed for starving men. I saw one man carrying round a dirty looking piece of meat and sharing it with his comrades. On making enquiries I was informed that it was part of a horse which had been killed when one of our aeroplanes dropped a bomb. They had half cooked it and were eating it with relish. I quite envied one man I saw walking about with the horse's jaw bone in his hands eating the meat off it. This was certainly more nourishing than soup.

During the day the Belgian Relief Committee brought into barracks a big box of soap cut up into small pieces. A small piece was served out to each of us and the majority had their first wash that day since their capture six or eight weeks ago. They had no towels and simply had to let the water dry on their faces and then stripped off their shirts to catch the creepers. They did not get into some quiet place to do it, for by this time we were all alike for the shavings we slept on were infected with lice.

Each day more men came into camp until our numbers including French, Belgians and Italians numbered 2,000. We had to be in our rooms every night by 8pm and were locked in. We passed the time by playing cards, etc. During my stay at Dendermonde a Belgian explained to me what the frontier was like. It was situated, he said, in a NE direction and 20 miles away. To get to it one would have to travel nearly all the time through a large wood. On the frontier there are three rows of wire. The first row is barbed wire entanglements, the second is single electric wires, seven in number and seven feet high. Beyond that is another barbed wire entanglement. The rows of wire are so placed that one would have to walk a considerable distance after getting past the wires before one got to the Dutch border. There are sentries on either side of the wire and placed 150 yards apart. I asked him how he knew the single wires were electric. He replied that rabbits were often found dead on it and sometimes men when they have been trying to escape. By means of a sketch drawn in the sand he explained to me where there was a hidden tunnel leading from Belgium into Holland and used for smuggling things, but another Belgian standing near at once contradicted this and said that the tunnel had recently been discovered and filled in by the Germans. He went on to say that some men had escaped by fixing a dry board to their backs and waiting for a very dark night had crawled under the wires without being electrocuted. You can also bribe the sentries, he continued, but this is a bit risky as they have been known to accept the bribe and shoot the man as he tried to get through the wire. You could, he said, rely on the help of the Belgians as any of them would help an Englishman escape, and even he went on to tell me where to go if I could get out of camp. There were however, powerful electric lights at every corner of the barrack square and sentries all around with loaded rifles, for they don't leave much to chance.

Amongst the prisoners were quite a number wearing the rank of Corporal or Sergeant, having put up their stripes since capture. One would not blame them for NCOs are not supposed to work whilst prisoners and perhaps some of the men knew this. Some went a little too far as quite young lads were wearing the rank of Company

Sergeant Major and looked ridiculous for so young a rating. Some of the prisoners, belonging to the Highland Regiments, were wearing kilts. They were not long in camp, however, before the kilts were exchanged for a pair of German trousers and 6 marks (5/-). There was about 7 yards of Scotch plaid in each kilt and the Germans would have no difficulty in selling it to the Belgians in the town for over a guinea a yard as cloth was both scarce and costly in Belgium. A pair of good army boots, which often went in exchange for a loaf of black bread, would fetch as much as £8 in town. A German NCO would often bring a loaf of black bread around the rooms and sell it for 3/-; where he got it from is another matter. Most of the Germans were wearing English khaki puttees and one day a German sent a Belgian to ask me if I would sell mine for 2 marks. *"No!"* I replied *"I would not sell them for 20 marks, and also tell him that I hate the sight of him and all his click."* Just at that moment I was feeling very hungry and wretched but I would not part with any of my clothing, not knowing where I should get the next from. To get money for buying bread I saw a man one day sell a solid gold watch for 20 marks. It must have cost anything up to £10 (a mark is worth 10d) A friend told me one day he was so hungry he had given his gold signet ring for a loaf of bread. The ring was a present from his wife just before he had left for France, and he said it nearly broke his heart to give it away. Many a brave fellow would be going home minus a ring or other present his mother or wife gave to him as a keepsake, and on being asked where it is they will say they lost it. Very few will tell their loved ones they were obliged to give them away for a bit of black bread.

One Thursday we had orders that we were to leave Dendermonde that night, but although they sent a strong guard down to escort us, we did not leave because there was no train available, all the trains being used for troops. We were then informed that we would go the next morning but Sunday and Monday passed and we still remained in the starvation camp. The German officer acknowledged that there was not enough food to keep us for a fortnight as arrangements had been made for only seven days, as very few prisoners stopped over that time, and 2,000 men, of course take a lot of feeding.

To give readers an idea of the system of feeding I will try to explain. Soup time was 12 noon and all men lined up in four groups, four deep, with NCOs in the ranks as Germans made no distinction and they were not allowed to keep the men in order. After waiting till 12.30 we are told the soup will be ready at 1 pm. Some of the men now fall out but others remain where they are so as to keep first place. At 1 pm we line up again and then the Germans start the painful business of counting us, going up and down the lines about a dozen times. If four Germans can count 2,000 men standing in columns of fours in under an hour it ought to be put up in letters of gold. At 2 pm the kitchen window is opened and they start serving out the water for it has by this time got to that. If you happen to be at the end of the line you are lucky to get your soup by 3 pm. This happened every day.

Owing to a Belgian escaping one day, the whole of us were locked in our rooms for two days and only allowed one hour's exercise each morning. Now for a bit of

German brutality. The order was given one day for us to go back into our rooms and some of the men were a bit slow in getting there. Those in rear got a few vicious kicks to help them along, and the Germans can kick very hard too, when they know you cannot retaliate. One of them who was doing most of the kicking was a little German about 4ft 6in in height and I could have picked him up and squeezed the life of him had I dared. I certainly felt like trying it. A Sergeant Major was among the last unlucky ones and of course he came in for the kicks. He requested to see the Commandant of the barracks but was not allowed so I presume the guards are allowed this sort of amusement. No doubt it is just as well to receive your punishment with a smile for one is apt to get shot for striking a guard.

One day a Sergeant was out of the ranks a little and a German came along and punched him. The Sergeant gave him one in return. Out came the German's bayonet in an instant and he made to drive it through the Sergeant but thought better of it, and after a lot of spluttering, for he was too angry to talk, he walked away. One Australian Corporal was one day going into his room when, for some unknown reason, he received a vicious kick from a German. The Corporal was well over 6ft and he turned to the German, but knowing the consequences, he checked himself just in time. *"Do that again"* he said to the German *"and I will ring your neck."* A big German guardsman saw the incident and riding across the parade on his cycle came up in rear of the Corporal and struck him a heavy blow on the back of the head, jumped back out of reach and drew a loaded revolver and with a grin on his face, stood at bay. With the remark *"You have won this time"* the Corporal went into his room.

Speaking to some of the men who had been working behind the German lines they told me some terrible news of their ill-treatment. When our planes came over the Germans would dart for cover and leave our lads to shift for themselves as best they could. Quite a number of our lads were killed by our own bombs and as these men were not registered as prisoners of war, their friends in England would never know the sufferings they endured. Can you give me a particular incident of one man being killed, I asked, *"Oh yes"* he said *"Private Bicknell of the 10th Royal Warwicks, who was in hospital having had both his legs blown off by a bomb dropped from one of our own planes. After 14 days in hospital he died. Just before he passed away he asked me to send his love to his loved ones at home and tell them how he died."* And so passed another murdered British hero for this man was quite well when he was captured.

Speaking one day to a Sergeant of the King's Liverpool Regiment he told me that for six weeks they had been shut up in Fort McDonald. 300 men were shut up in one room which was 75ft long by 21ft wide. They were only allowed out to draw their food. They were not allowed any water to wash or drink, and some of them washed their faces in their coffee. There was only one small window in the room and they called it *'The Black Hole of Fort McDonald'*.

On 26th June we were ordered to fall in outside and after having our names called we were told we would leave that night for Germany. Should an order be passed for 469 party to fall we must fall in at once. We returned our bowls and blankets during the forenoon and fell in ready for marching off at 8pm that night. The usual part of Germans was detailed off to count us and they could not get the correct number till 10pm. About 75 Germans surrounded us with loaded rifles and fixed bayonets and several officers pranced around on horses shouting orders to their men. The Belgian who had just been captured after escaping was made to join up with our party. Half a loaf of bread was served out to each man and we had the order to march at 10.30pm. We passed through the ruins of Dendermonde on our way to the station. Although it was quite late a good many Belgians stood at their doors to see us off, some waved to us and shouted farewell messages.

After a good many halts for the men were not very strong and lagged behind, we finally got to the station at 11.30pm. Standing on a siding was an engine and a long trail of cattle trucks. There were 1,500 men and it took a considerable time for us to entrain. 36 men were put in each truck and two German sentries with them. There were a few seats in the trucks, but we were hopelessly crowded to be anything like comfortable. The two doors were left open to give us air and the two Germans sat facing out of the trucks with their loaded rifles between their knees. Some who were lucky lay prone on the floor and went to sleep but others had to sleep in the sitting position.

With a jerk the train left at 3am the next morning and we started on our way to Germany, passing through some of the most beautiful scenery in Belgium. It was haymaking time and everyone was busy in the fields. What struck me as peculiar was that most of the hay was cut with scythes and I only saw one mowing machine on the whole journey through Belgium and Germany. The crops were exceptionally good everywhere. German soldiers in large numbers were working in some fields getting in the hay. Our guards told us we would get some soup at 8am that morning on reaching one of the stations, but we got nothing until we reached Bansteig at 1pm and then we were given a drink of coffee only.

We reached Aachen at 6pm where soup was supposed to be given us, but at this place we had a drop of coffee each and a thin slice of black bread, but even that was welcome as we had only the quarter of a loaf for that day. Some of our men were so hungry they had eaten both days rations as soon as they got it and went hungry for the rest of the journey. We passed through Baal, Erkelenz and Munchen Gladbach and at midnight we stopped at a small station and were given a bowl of soup which was very sour, known as sauerkraut by many prisoners of war. We were hungry enough to eat it however, and it certainly filled us even if it didn't fatten us.

We arrived at a place called Haltern at 6.30am on 28th June and were told we had to detrain and form up for marching off, so we had arrived in Germany at last. Haltern is only a very small town and as we marched through the streets I could not help but notice the very unhappy looks of the German people who were thin and war weary, many a scornful look we had as we passed on our journey. There was not a particle of food exhibited in any shop window. A cycle passed us with spring tyres which amused us very much indeed. Round the rim, instead of rubber, was a concoction of springs. It was quite unnecessary for any of the cycles to have bells on their handlebars for the noise of the springs could be heard quite a long way off. Tired and hungry as we were our march seemed a long one, the distance to the camp being seven miles. We had a few rests by the roadside and finally reached Dülman camp at 9am on 28th June.

Dülman

We halted in the road leading to the camp and after being counted, the French and Italians were separated from us and taken to some other part of the camp. We now got into single file and as we went through the gate in the barbed wire we were given a basin, spoon and card. The camp is a large one with accommodation for 50,000 men. It is built of wooden huts and separated into compounds with four huts in each compound with a cook house and water closet. Round each compound is barbed wire and round the whole camp are more rows of barbed wire 10ft high. Outside the wire are sentries with loaded rifles and fixed bayonets placed 50 yards apart. There are many powerful electric lights which are turned on at night time and throw rays of light all around the wire. The camp is situated in the heart of the country seven miles from the small town of Haltern and four miles from Dülman, another small town. It is only 16 miles from the Dutch frontier. Surrounding one half of the camp is a large wood and the other half is flat open country with a single railway line running between the two towns, and wide open roads.

We were now ordered to fill in our cards with the following details, Rank, Name, Regiment, Trade, where born and date and where captured. We had to fill in these cards as quickly as possible and then hand them in. Sergeants and above were separated from the rest and asked if we were all qualified Sergeants. Of course everyone replied 'Yes'. We were then asked by the German officer to produce our pay cards. The men who had promoted themselves had Private on their paybooks, but some were wary enough to say they had lost their books. The men who had Private in their books were put back with the other men and the men who had no paybooks the Germans wanted witnesses to say they were qualified NCOs. Of course there were plenty of witnesses. Corporals were mustered next, but by this time the rumour had got around and self-promoted Corporals, when they were mustered had all lost their books and had witnesses ready. Stretcher bearers and RAMC men were also separated from the rest.

We were given some good soup at 1pm and then a German Sergeant said we would all go into our compounds that afternoon. *"You must not"* he said *"take any money into the camp, English money and German money will be changed for prison money. If any man is caught with proper money on him after this he will be severely punished."* Of course with prison money one cannot bribe sentries or buy anything outside the camp should one escape. That afternoon we went round the various changers' tables and for German notes we were given paper money of the same value except that it had the word *Kriegsgefangenenlager* on the front and the name of the camp on the back. Notes were printed as low as one pfennig, which is equal to a tenth of a penny.

We were told off in batches of 36 and each batch marched off into an enclosed compound taking our few belongings with us. In the centre of the compound were three tables and at each table sat two German NCOs, whose business was to thoroughly search our pockets and bundles. My thoughts instantly went to my book, for of course to be able to write this book I had to have notes. I had jotted down in shorthand everything I had been through and my little black book was half filled with notes. It was in my top left hand pocket. I sneaked to the rear and my friend stood directly in front of me while I took the book out of my pocket, undid my puttees, put the book in my sock and fastened the puttees round my leg again. My turn came to be searched, my bundle was gone through first and they took out just what they wanted, my pockets were systematically searched and the least scrap of paper with writing on was carefully put on one side. Even my prayer book, because a friend had written three of four words on it was taken but they forgot to search my puttees.

Before I proceed any further I would like to say that although I was searched a good many times after this during my stay in Germany I always managed to get my little black book safely through. If readers have ever noticed a soldiers khaki tunic they know that on either side of the chest is an extra piece of khaki cloth and the top seam of each is under the shoulder strap. By undoing the shoulder strap and cutting this seam it formed a pocket big enough to put my book in, and by fastening the shoulder strap again it hid the top very nicely. Every time I was searched my book went into this pocket and the Germans never thought of putting their hands up there and I was able to bring it safely home to England.

The things that were taken off us were put in a heap at the end of the table. If a man had a good jersey, socks, flannel or pocket knife these were taken off him. By this time there were not many watches or jewellery, or that may have been taken as well. The spoil was no doubt shared out afterwards. I am not going to say that this sort of thieving was sanctioned by the German authorities but nevertheless it happened each time a new batch of prisoners came in and I expect quite a lot of money was made out of the swindle. What was left in our bundles was not much good, but these had to be taken to a German and a label put on them and a check with a number on it was given to the owner. I don't know if the German in charge of these bundles thought that it was a wonderful thing to be honest, but to each man he gave a check with the words "*I am quite honest and will not rob your bundles.*"

We were now taken to a large shed and on getting inside we were told to take our clothes off, tie them together and hang them on some hooks on a trolley. As the nights had been cold I was wearing a double shift of underclothing and a jersey and put them all on the hook. Our boots and braces we carried in our hands. The trolley was now pushed in a big tank and a terrific heat turned on to fumigate the clothes and kill the livestock. While this was taking place we went into the barbers shop where three Englishmen and one German with a pair of clippers each cut off every bit of hair on our heads and bodies, and we looked some guys by the time they had finished with us. We next went into another room where three shower baths were turned on and you washed as well as you could. A miserable bit of rag was given to you to wipe on and then a bully with a stick drove us like cattle into another room. Some grey ointment was given us and we were made to smear it over our bodies. After half an hour's wait in a warm room the trolley with the fumigated clothes came out all steaming hot, but by a curious coincidence some of the best of our underclothing had mysteriously disappeared. For instance my extra shift had gone, the best of it, of course. A Sergeant Major lost a new jersey and quite a lot of men had lost the best they had on their backs. You now took your remaining underclothing to a German who gave you in exchange a shirt and a pair of drawers that were disgustingly dirty and ragged. On these ragged articles the word 'Dülman' was stamped.

Whilst we lined up to exchange things three or four Germans went round the remainder of our clothes and robbed us while we looked on. Oh yes, the curs were armed, they always are, and that saves argument. Thanks to the ladies of Bruges we had quite a nice lot of underclothing, but after these robbers were finished, we just had a dirty shirt and a pair of drawers and no socks. They will not allow us to complain to higher authorities. On getting outside the German in charge of our bundles handed them back to us with a 'told you so' look on his face, and to give him his due they had not been touched.

I managed to keep my gold watch which by the way was a German one, given to me by a German prisoner of war in the Cameroons for showing him a little kindness. The men belonging to the Navy were now ordered to fall out, and our number comprised 6 marines, 2 sailors, and we were marched off to a separate compound. The compound, boarded all round with boards 10ft high, had accommodation for 500 men. All round the huts was about two feet of sand. In the compound are 400 French soldiers and we were informed we would stay here at least 14 days. In the rooms were strips of coconut matting stretched out between pieces of wood and two thin blankets (not over clean) at the foot of each and comprised our beds.

Routine and food. We turn out each day at 5.30am and two men go for the black coffee substitute which is our breakfast. The water is now turned on in the wash house for one hour during which time you have a wash and scrub the wash house and WCs clean. At 7am we fall in for muster getting four deep. A French Sergeant Major calls the whole lot up to attention, and going up to a German Private who is in charge of the compound, salutes him, and reports present or otherwise. As we were only a small party, we guess the orders of the French Sergeant Major and drill with them. The German Private now counts us over and then tells certain men to rake over the sand and pick up paper, etc. At 12 noon we get a basin of soup made with mangolds and nothing else. After dinner you try to sleep off your hunger until 5pm when you get another basin of the same stuff and two thin slices of bread. In the evening we were mustered again and so our miserable existence continued.

On the walls of the huts were various writings which told only too truly how others had suffered the pangs of hunger. Such things as *'Oh Roll on that parcel from Blighty, will it never come?'* and *'To Hell with starvation.'* There was also a good drawing of the Kaiser swinging from the gallows. We had not been in the compound very long before some emergency parcels were served out to us. One parcel between two men. The parcel consisted of 3 tins of corned beef, 1 veal loaf, 4 packets of biscuits, 1 tin of cheese, 1 tin of dripping, 1 packet of cocoa and 1 packet of tea. We were told we would get one every seven days, but although we were at this camp for over 10 weeks, we only had three parcels all the time. Stocks of emergency parcels are sent to each prisoner of war camp to be distributed amongst men who are not in receipt of parcels from England, but as so many thousands of English prisoners were captured during the great advance, the men soon cleared the stocks out, and it is six weeks before other parcels can be sent across the frontier which the Germans have a nasty knack of closing during certain times of the year.

What very few parcels we did get however helped us out a little and we made them last as long as we could. I think I am quite right in saying, had it not been for these parcels very few prisoners would have seen England again and what few did come back could never have built up again. Speaking from personal experience I was, after 12 weeks on German diet, very weak and depressed, and it was only strong will power that kept me from breaking down altogether. I see, according to English newspapers, that many thousands of English prisoners could not be accounted for. Let me say that those men who were not killed whilst working behind German lines, have been systematically starved to death in the prison camps of Germany and a good many little wooden crosses will be found in Dülman camp. I defy any man to live on a small piece of black bread and two lots of mangold soup a day. The composition of the bread being potatoes, rye and sawdust. I have a piece of it at home to prove it.

Thinking we would be forced to work, I thought of volunteering to work on a farm as I was brought up to that sort of work, but the English Sergeant Major at the camp passed the order round that owing to an arrangement between the British and German governments, Corporals and above should not be made to work. We were informed that if we volunteered the Germans would at once report to the British government to that effect, and all pay due to us would be stopped at once and we would be court-martialled on getting home. Of course no one volunteered after that although the Germans asked NCOs to volunteer, promising them good jobs. Lance Corporals and Privates were, however, made to work and quite a number of them were working at their respective trades in the camp. Men who had been miners had to work down the mines, a good many of which were in the district; for this work they received the magnificent sum of 4d a day and a little extra bread.

During our stay at Dülman we were inoculated five times and vaccinated once. It was not optional. We would strip to the waist and file into a room where one man would give you a dab with an iodine brush and then you would go across to another German who, with a phial and needle, would give you a prod with it in the left breast, and without attempting to disinfect the needle would do two or three others until his phial was empty. So if any man was suffering from any disease another man was likely to catch it. After everyone was finished we would line up and the German doctor would walk along the ranks and if the iodine smudge was there you had been inoculated. He little thought at the time that some of us would be artful enough to transfer the iodine off one man's breast with the aid of our finger and smear our own. By this means I escaped inoculation three times. Personally I am a firm believer in the system of inoculation but I like to know what with, and what for, and there was a rumour going round that the enemy was inoculating us with consumptive germs.

I witnessed a rather amusing incident one day during inoculation. There was an English doctor in the camp and he was assisting the German doctor. Of course our lads edged up to the English doctor to be done and avoided the German who had to keep telling our men to come to him. The German had just filled his phial and shouted to the man in front of me to go to him. The man hesitated and the German was so angered that he caught the man by the arm and with extra force drove the needle into the man's flesh. The needle broke off at the joint and the matter squirted all over the German's face. The man walked out of the room, not having seen what happened, with the needle still stuck in his chest. The doctor, having regained his speech, rushed after the man and took the needle out.

The first week at the camp we had the martial law read to us. All the new arrivals were formed up into a square and the Camp Commandant took his place in the centre. An English speaking German read the rules very carefully over to us. You must not damage crops or your barracks. You must not mutiny or incite to mutiny. If you have a knowledge of such you must report it. You must obey all orders at once. No matter what rank you are a German Private is your superior and you must salute him. For committing any of the above crimes the penalty is death or 5 to 15 years close confinement in a Fortress. After reading these orders the Commandant asked if anyone did not understand these orders they should step out to the front and they will be fully explained. Next day the rules were brought round for each man to sign his name to.

The Germans were very particular about one's uniform. We were, of course, in khaki, but our steel helmets had been given away or taken off us and most men were wearing civilian hats. Those in possession of hats had to go to the tailor's shop and have a yellow triangular piece of cloth sewn on top, and so that you could not take it off, the cap was cut away underneath the patch. Some of the men were wearing civilian suits but these were taken off them and they were given 'prisoner of war' uniform, which is a blue suit with wide yellow stripes down the trouser legs and a wide yellow band round the left arm. These clothes are sent out from England and each prisoner, if he is lucky, gets a complete kit after being a prisoner for 6 months. I said lucky because quite a number of the men had cards to say the clothes were despatched from England, but the poor fellows never received them. I was amongst that number.

In our room there were 50 French Sergeants and we got very friendly with them. The system of their government feeding them seemed to me the best way. All their foodstuffs were sent in bulk from France and not parcels sent to individual men as ours was sent. Each French soldier gets a weekly ration of 50 large biscuits, a bag of rice, box of raisins, tin of dripping, tea, sugar, beans and bacon. The French were very good to us and very often would give us things when we were getting low, although they had none too much themselves. One of the Sergeants could speak a very little English and it was astonishing how he improved as the days dragged by. One day he asked us where we were captured and we told him Zeebrugge. No sooner had we said that than he shouted something to his chums in French and they gathered round. He told us they were all captured before April, but had heard all about Zeebrugge but would we explain what really happened. By means of boxes and drawings we finally got them to understand although it took us nearly three hours to explain the operation. So interested were they in the operation that they stood about in groups discussing it for hours afterwards. These 400 Frenchmen under a French Sergeant Major were very well disciplined and spotlessly clean. The Germans hated them and the least excuse was good enough to get them punished. The French knew this and of course gave no trouble. On the bugle blowing the fall in, they would drop what they were doing and rush to fall in. We were on parade and the French Sergeant Major had just called us to attention. Two Frenchmen had not got their heels close enough together. That was enough the old German Private. He went white with passion, shouted and gesticulated, talking of course in his own language and then finally got hold of the men by their coats, dragged them to the front and made them stand to attention facing us, whilst we stood at ease. This rather tickled us but we dare not smile.

After 14 days in this compound we were removed to another where there were 200 Englishmen. We were now allowed to write home and send our address, and replies could be sent to this camp as it was a registered one. We had, of course, written home before but the address at the top had been inked over and they could not reply. We were also officially registered as prisoners of war and our names sent through to England for parcels. If a British Tommie gets a letter or parcel from England during the first five months of his capture he is very lucky indeed. I waited five months and three weeks for my first letter from England and six months for my first and only parcel, despite the fact that six per month were sent to me from the Navy League commencing from 23rd August.

150 men were sorted out for work and those who were sick were sent to another compound. They were fallen in next day and were given to understand they were to work down the mines. Each man was

A group of British prisoners fall in prior to being marched off for a bath, with their German guards, most of whom were elderly soldiers unfit for service on the Western Front

served out with the following articles; greatcoat, shirt, drawers and toe rags (which was nothing more than two pieces of flannel wrapped around the feet to act as socks). Each man was also given a pair of clogs (just pieces of wood with holes cut for the feet to go in). I offered my services to help serve the things out so that the men should not be kept on parade too long. In serving the shirts out I gave an Australian a shirt much too small for him. He was a big man and when he held it up he looked so ridiculous I went back at once and sorted out a bigger one to give him. The German saw me do this, walked over to me, shook his fist in my face and shouted something in German which I understood to mean that I had committed a crime and would be punished for it. I served out the other few shirts I had and took good care never to volunteer for anything else.

After these men left, and the sick as well, there was only nine of us left so we got into one of the little rooms and made it nice and clean. We had no sooner got it clean than we had orders to move into another compound and the room we were now put in had a mixture of French, Portuguese, Russians, Italians, Belgians and one of two Rumanians, the remainder being British. The room was disgustingly dirty, the dirt being three inches thick under the beds. The bed I was allotted was swarming with fleas, and as I am not friendly with these jumping insects, I had no sleep all the time I was in that room. I did everything to get rid of them by putting my blankets and bed daily on the lines and beating them.

In this room was an Englishman who had just done 15 months in a German prison. His story was that he had been taken prisoner two years earlier and whilst he was in Belgium he managed to escape. He went to Brussels where he got a passport and with this he was able to travel round Belgium, the people assisting him. He lived as best he could and after seven months he resorted to thieving and pickpocketing to get money when he was a bit low, until he was finally captured and sent to prison. On being asked if he had ever tried to get across the frontier he said he was quite happy enough in Belgium. He could speak English but he certainly couldn't write it. I was rather puzzled over this and asked the English doctor his opinion of it, and in rather strong words he informed me that the man was nothing more than a German spy, dressed as an English prisoner and put amongst us to get information. I at once informed my comrades and put them on their guard.

I was rather surprised one day when a German came into the room and asked for Sergeant Wright. He told me I was wanted in the office and on getting there I found two Germans. The one who was an officer sat behind a desk strewn with papers, and another I was not supposed to see, was screened off in a corner of a room ready to take down in writing anything I said. *"I have just sent for you Sergeant to have a quiet chat. I daresay you get a bit bored in camp sometimes, don't you."* "Yes" I replied quite nicely for I was determined to be friendly with him. *"How do you like this camp?"* he asked. *"Oh fairly well"* I replied *"One doesn't expect feather beds and bacon and eggs whilst a prisoner of war."* *"Well we do everything to make your lives comfortable"* he said with a leer. Looking him straight in the eyes I said *"I take it for granted you belong to the Intelligence Staff and sent for me to get information."* He was rather taken aback but recovering himself said *"Oh no

Sergeant, nothing of the kind. I am not clever enough to belong to that branch and only sent for you to ask if you are a marine why are you dressed in khaki as we cannot quite understand it and we are thinking of sending you to Brandenburg naval camp." "*We changed from blue into khaki*" I replied "*just for the operation and had we got back we would be in blue now.*"

"*Who do you think will win the war?*" he continued after we had chatted for a long time. "*Why we will of course*" I replied quite good humouredly. "*My dear fellow*" he said "*our submarines alone will win the war for us and you being a navy man must surely know that.*" Now was my chance. "*Don't you be too sure*" I replied "*for we have your submarine warfare well in hand. We are capturing your submarines, taking them to England, putting English crews on board and sending them to sea as decoys.*" Whilst I was saying this he sat back in his chair, opened his mouth and looked at me as if I had gone mad. The other man in the corner was busy writing.

"*Are you sure of this Sergeant?*" "*Absolutely certain of it*" I replied. "*When I was in England it was common knowledge amongst the British public and I daresay your Intelligence Staff in Berlin know all about it. Another thing which is also well known in England is that every Merchant ship which goes to sea is fitted with an instrument that can detect a submarine at a distance of two miles so your argument falls flat when you say you can win the war with your submarines.*" "*You have given me a great surprise this afternoon Sergeant*" he said "*and I am rather surprised at an English NCO giving an enemy such splendid information. I can assure you that the Intelligence Staff in Berlin knows nothing about this, but they will know very shortly. Thank you very much.*" With a grievous look on my face I said "*I hope you will keep this information from my superiors in England or I shall get into serious trouble.*" "*That will be alright Sergeant*" he replied "*How are you looking for smokes. Have these*" and he gave me a huge handful of cigarettes and cigars.

I then told him I had a chum very ill in hospital and asked if I could go to see him. He agreed and told a German NCO to go and get a passport from the office so I left him with these words ringing in his ears. "*Good afternoon Sergeant, and thank you*" and I expect he thought what a poor thing I was. Of course I never mentioned this conversation to anyone afterwards, not even to my dearest chum, but I hardly expected the German officer to swallow the pill so easily without trying to trip me up in further arguments.

My friend in hospital was an Engine Room Artificer who had been in the Zeebrugge raid on the *Vindictive* and got safely back to England. He was one of the volunteers later to come again on the *Vindictive* to Ostend when she sank herself in the canal. There were two prisoners taken during that operation and he was one of them. He was swimming about in the water for some time with his lifebelt on and then when the fire ceased he made his way to the pier and hung on to one of the stanchions until he was discovered next morning. Through being in the water all night he caught a very bad cold and without medical attention it developed to something else, until one day he was taken off to hospital. To pass the miserable hours away I had been teaching him Pitman's shorthand and this of course, developed into a strong friendship.

The ward he was in looked anything but comfortable. There were 40 beds in the ward most of which had English patients. There was a Frenchman in charge of the ward. The beds were made of wood but the blankets and sheets were not a bit clean. My friend was looking very ill but very cheerful indeed and said he felt much better. The German sat with me whilst I was talking to him and after half an hour I was told I must go. I shook hands with my friend and that was the last time I saw him.

As I have mentioned before, we had an English doctor in the camp and he was the only British officer we had. He was very rarely allowed in the hospital and his duty was attending to the slight cases which were put in special huts about the camp. He was a very nice fellow and all the boys were fond of him. No man ever did more to ease the sufferings of starving and unhappy men. Quite a number of the lads had discharging wounds and the doctor was greatly handicapped because of lack of Red Cross stores. He informed us that on getting to the camp that over £150 of Red Cross stores were missing from the camp, which should have been there on his arrival. Our lads, especially those who had been working behind the lines, were in a very bad state and quite a number of them were dying daily. The doctor told me one day that had he not seen the men with his own eyes he would not have believed that men could have got into such a low condition and still live. *"Why"* he continued *"they are living skeletons and those who have died have died from starvation."* I don't think any doctor had a more painful duty than he had, to see his own countrymen dying of starvation and not be able to put out a helping hand. Surely this should not happen after four years of war. Men should not have to wait three months before they can receive an emergency parcel and five months for a parcel from home. Quite a number of lads killed themselves by eating too much of their parcel when they got it, their stomachs being too weak.

After a short time in this compound we were sent to another but not before being searched for information and notebooks, but nothing was taken off me this time. We were put in a room with 50 privates of various regiments. The 'Spanish grip' had broken out in camp by this time and the doctor and his assistants were kept busy. Quite a number of the poor fellows in this hut had got it. They were too weak to leave their beds (coconut matting and 2 blankets). They simply lay there and suffered, one man who occupied the bed under me just lay in his bed for over a week with his head under his blanket the whole time, with the exception of the time he was eating his food. His body was covered with bed sores and he looked an object of misery. Those who were too weak to fight against it simply died.

Arguments would sometimes develop into a fight and it would be really funny to see two men, almost too weak to stand, trying to fight one another. It certainly caused much amusement to the others although it was a pathetic sight. After a few minutes fighting they would be utterly exhausted but neither of them would even be bruised. After a week in this hut the NCOs were sent to another compound where all the NCOs had been put together. We were rather sorry to be separated from the other four marines, as one of them had the grips and was very ill. Naturally we stood by one another in illness and did what little we could for those who were ill.

The room we now went to was full of Sergeants and Corporals some of whom were in receipt of parcels from England. Being NCOs and not having to work, the Germans reduced our rations and instead of having two slices of bread per day we only had one. This slice of bread was 5 inches long, 4 inches wide and ½ inch thick, and four days out of seven we had mangold soup. Had these mangolds been fresh from the fields as we see them in England, it would not have been too bad, but the stuff we had was mangolds cut into slices about 1 inch long and had been put into barrels and kept from the year before, and the soup stank by the time we got it. As vile as it was we had to eat it or die. By this time we were getting so weak some of us could not walk to the washhouse twice a day to have a wash. Of course it may have been the 'Spanish grip' we had but I will leave it to the reader to judge.

There were about 20 men in this room who were in receipt of parcels from England and were getting six a month regularly. These men were living quite well on their parcels and the majority had a big stock in hand. It was very hard on the rest of us, who were starving, to watch the others each meal time having a good tuck into bully beef, biscuits, etc. I was in this hut about six weeks and I only saw two men out of 20 give anything away, and there were men in this hut too ill to stand and not even a cup of tea was given them. I am afraid our comments on the English system of parcelling was not very favourable especially when some of the men were selling their German bread to their starving comrades for half a mark a slice. This is quite true and a great many English prisoners will hold with this statement. No doubt they were quite right in saying they must put some by for a rainy day in case the frontier was closed and their parcels stopped, and of course they had starved like us until their parcels arrived, but the French system seemed to be far the best for everyone.

The sanitary arrangements in the camp were fairly good but the men were too weak to get to the proper places and we had to live under the most disgusting conditions. If we asked the Germans for cleaning material for the huts they would laugh with the words 'You English swine' – in fact every order they gave finished up with those words. 'Nix arbeit, Nix Essen' (No work, no food) was another thing they often liked to taunt us with.

The privates that were well enough were marched off at 6am each day and made to work in the fields amongst the potatoes and cabbages, and of course they came back in the evening with their pockets full and brought back some sticks to cook them with. The fellows down the mines, however, had some awful tales to tell. They certainly got a little extra bread but it was very heavy work for the half famished men. Many a kick they got to help them on, or a club with a rifle, and one or two were shot. One of the punishments if they did not work hard enough was to make them stand on a single brick for two hours with a sentry in front of them with a loaded rifle, and a greater punishment was two days imprisonment without food. A party of 50 NCOs were taken to a pit one day. They were not told anything about it until they arrived there. They knew they were not supposed to work and despite the fact that the Germans tried to bribe them, they absolutely refused to work, so after five days starvation they were brought back to camp again.

After six weeks we were given an Emergency parcel each and we made this last a fortnight with a little care, and it was astonishing how quickly we picked up again and got a little stronger, The German in charge of the cookhouse would give 11 pieces of bread for a tin of corned beef and nine pieces for one packet of tea. He did quite a trade. The Germans were allowed so much bread for each compound and by cutting the slices very thin he made quite a lot out of the transaction. When he could not get corned beef or tea then he would sell the bread for one mark (10d) a slice and our boys were only too pleased to buy it. Had I had the money I would have bought it also as hunger is a terrible thing.

Each man had a card with his prison number, name and regiment on it. He was obliged to have this on his person at all times. Men would be punished for trifling offences for instance. We were fallen in on parade one day, a Sergeant had a button undone. The German Sergeant went up to him and demanded his card. This card was taken to the Commandant of the camp and the case explained by the German, but the Sergeant whose card was taken was not allowed to see him. Seven weekends in cells was the punishment for this awful crime, so every Friday night this NCO was locked in a little cell until Monday morning. Laughing on parade was another terrible crime and one NCO got 10 weekends for that.

Clogs were served out to us and we had orders to give our boots to the Germans. Some did give them in but others wore the clogs and hid their boots. Of course it was possible to escape from Dülman as the Dutch border was only 16 miles away. Quite a number of Frenchmen did escape and manage to get over the border into Holland and safely home. They would select some dark cover, cut the wire and bolt into the wood. The German sentries fired sometimes but very rarely hit any of them. Armed with reliable sketches and compasses the escapees always seemed to be successful. These French sketches were always well guarded and no Englishman could approach them on the subject. How they got the sketches and compasses I leave the reader to guess. It was also possible to bribe some of the German sentries.

The English also had a sketch which was secretly passed round the camp and given to anyone who thought of escaping. Every detail of the surrounding country was there, brooks, woods, railway towns, etc. The position of sentries were also marked. Accompanying the sketch were full instructions telling you the best way to go and how and where to cross the frontier. Our sketch was not guarded like the French sketch and it was quite easy for anyone to get a copy, and some of us had the idea that both the sketch and instructions had been put round the camp by the German authorities. At least 10 of our boys escaped from the camp but the majority were caught at a small town called Ahern and none of them crossed the border. One man was unlucky enough to get shot by the sentries on the frontier. This man's body was put into a coffin, a photograph taken and stuck up on the notice boards for all to see. The men that were caught were brought back to the camp and taken before the Commandant, but the old man was very reasonable. If the men cut the wire in getting out of camp they were given seven days in cells for damaging prison property and seven days for trying to escape. *"It is your duty to escape"* said the Commandant *"but it is also the duty of my sentries to shoot and kill you if they see you escaping"*.

We had taken up the floor in one of the huts near the barbed wire and with the aid of cardboard boxes, we had built a tunnel going under the wire and it should have opened out into the wood had not a German sentry fallen through it one day. The tunnel had been built at night and taken weeks to do it as the sand had to be carried outside and strewn about, dodging the German sentries in the meantime. It was very interesting work and such a pity that it was discovered. When it was found none of us knew anything about it and it may have been there for years for all we knew.

The German sentries would often converse with us over the wire, and we were talking to one of them one night and he told us he had spent nearly all his time in England and his wife, an Englishwoman was still there. *"Look here lads"* he said quite unexpectedly *"I am quite willing the next time I am at this post to let two of you escape, and come with you myself to the frontier and get you safely across into Holland. Only you must tell the Dutch authorities that I did everything to assist you. I hate this country, England is the place for me."* Two of us kept a sharp look out for that sentry each night but he never turned up again and we heard later that he had been sent to the front.

If the Germans had any idea that there were maps and compasses about they would give an order for everyone to fall in outside and march us off to be thoroughly searched; In the meantime the huts, beds and bundles would be gone through, but although this happened very often nothing was found. Many a sketch however was quickly buried in the sand. We often got news that an organised search was about to take place and all documents were hidden or destroyed.

The German NCOs in charge of the compounds would often get very angry especially if the news was bad, and it was always advisable to obey their orders smartly. For instance an English Sergeant Major was a bit slow one day in obeying an order. The German at once drew his bayonet and stabbed the Sergeant Major in the back just missing one of his lungs. He was carried off to hospital and our English doctor saw the Camp Commandant but he got no satisfaction.

I was speaking to the doctor one day and was asked by him where I was captured and on being told, he said that he would like a quiet talk with me on the subject and asked if I would go up to his room that evening and tell him all about it. About 8pm I went up and found him at home. He had a comfortable little room compared with the rest of the camp. I was rather surprised when he locked the door, bunged the keyhole up and drew the screen over the window. *"One cannot be too careful, Sergeant"* he said *"and the camp is full of spies, and you know as a doctor I am not supposed to be interested in military affairs."* We got into conversation and I told him the full details about Zeebrugge. *"Now look here Sergeant, you are British NCO and trained to use your powers of observation. Did you notice the defences of Zeebrugge?"* *"Oh yes"* I replied *"I would like to get it through but I don't know how."* *"Leave that to me"* he said *"you understand shorthand as I can see from your book. I will give you some very thin paper and I want you to write all the information in shorthand so that it can be read, condense it to the smallest possible space possible, and report sick tomorrow morning and secretly pass it on to me. Mind you, Sergeant, not a word to anyone for if it leaks out it means the firing squad and a brick wall for both of us."* I assured him I would take care. I was always writing and the men took no notice of me that evening as I carefully wrote my information on the thin paper mentioning every detail of the defences. Next morning I reported sick and the doctor seeing me outside with the other man said "Well and what is the matter with you?" "Pain in the chest" I replied, so I stripped off, went inside and was examined. He shut the door and without speaking I passed my information to him. After giving me medical advice so that the men outside could hear, I departed on my way. I had another opportunity of speaking to him later and asked how he got the information through. *"I must leave you to guess"* he replied *"but you know empty medical stores are sent across the border to Copenhagen, and your information is in England by this time and everything is alright. Any time you think of escaping, come to me and I will give you a prismatic compass, two days' supply of chocolate and a genuine sketch,"* but being in such a weak condition I never felt like doing the journey.

There were about 20,000 prisoners in the camp and amongst these men was plenty of talent. We had our own band, the instruments having been sent out from England, and as there were professional actors amongst the men, we would arrange a concert once a week. There was a large hall set apart for our amusement but as this would only accommodate 500 men, the compounds had to go in turn. We also had cinema shows but we were obliged to sit and look at German pictures. One night a picture was being shown of a boat race between an Englishman and a German. It was a good race, but the German won. Our lads had followed the race with great interest and being rather disappointed about the German winning, they all shouted *"Never mind England, you're not beaten yet."* The Germans stopped the remaining pictures and ordered everyone outside, and arrested the senior Sergeant Major who was in charge of the entertainments committee. On getting outside he tried to hand his friends some documents but was not quick enough and the Germans got them. He was put under close arrest and a week later we saw him being marched away from camp. We would never find out what became of him or what charge was brought against him.

In addition to being in charge of the entertainments he was also head of the parcels committee and we had every reason to believe he had done his work well. This meant selecting another president and the NCOs had a meeting and selected one, but the Germans rejected him and wished to select one themselves. The doctor was handed over the keys until we came to some agreement. The NCOs got very discontented to think that the Germans should have so much influence over the Red Cross. Rumours went round the camp that there was a gigantic swindle going on as we were supposed to get an emergency parcel once every 10 days and we had only two in eight weeks, we began to think it was true when we were not allowed to select our own member who we knew was straight. Things now began to look very threatening and Sergeant Majors were asking permission to write to the Red Cross at Copenhagen for accounts, so the German authorities thought it best to send all NCOs, some 950 of us, to another camp as soon as possible.

On 20th August we were all mustered alphabetically and marched off to another compound where we were served out with a blue coat with a yellow band round the left arm, one shirt, clogs and toe rags. We each had to sign a paper to the effect that we had been given these articles. A stock of emergency parcels had just arrived in the camp and the doctor, who was now temporary president, saw that each man was given a parcel to go away with. We now had the painful duty of standing about five hours whilst each man was thoroughly searched and then we went back to our huts. At 2am next morning we had orders to go on parade and the roll was called again. As each man's name was called, he went to a German and handed in two blankets, a bowl, spoon and towel. He went through the gate in the compound, was handed tree thin slices of bread and finally reached the road where we formed up ready for marching off.

A very strong guard formed up all around the men, and each man was searched again as he went into the road. I had in my possession a piece of hoop iron which I had made into a knife. At the top was two pieces of wood bound round with cloth and string to use as a handle. It was a rusty old thing which would bend before it cut. Of course we were not allowed to carry knives and when I was searched this fearful instrument was found on me. The German became quite angry saying the words *"Verboten, Englander."* He took it across to the German NCO in charge of the search party and when he saw it he burst into laughter and ordered him to give it back to me.

We were counted over six times and finally started on our weary march to the station which was about four miles away. I shall always remember that walk and so will a good many more. We went extremely slowly and had a good many halts. The German officer shouted and spoke angry words in German but it was all to no purpose, the lads would not be hurried. We had plenty of stalwart German guards all around us with loaded rifles and fixed bayonets but a quarter of the number would have been plenty to have escorted that half famished crowd of men.

We reached Dülman at last and had to pass through the town to reach the station. It is a very small town but very pretty, having some fine old buildings, but not a particle of food was exhibited in any of the shop windows. It was early morning and we met the people going to work, most of them were women. There were quite a lot of cripples about and a big percentage of the young girls were hunch-backed and delicate. We arrived at the station and were rather surprised to see a train of carriages instead of cattle trucks. We were ordered to get six in a carriage and this gave us plenty of room.

At 9am the train moved off but we were not told where our destination was. We passed through Bosenell, Munster, Osnabrück, Hameln and Nordstemmen. Here we had our first meal having arrived at 5.45pm. We went into a large building with tables and stools and filed round a counter where three women gave us a bowl of soup, very good compared with the Dülman rubbish. It consisted of cabbage, potatoes and was flavoured with some kind of meat. Some of us were very fortunate enough to get some coffee to take into the carriage with us, for it was very hot and we got thirsty.

DÜLMAN

There was a magnificent monastery near this town with beautiful towers and situated on top of a hill. All around it was vast woods with ornamental bridges over a stream. A few sharp orders from our guards and we were soon entrained again and on our way. The enemy's crops en route were exceptionally good but very few people were working in the fields. It was beautiful weather and some of the crops were quite fit to gather in. Rather a pretty incident happened at one of the German stations, where a big crowd of civilians were on the platforms. A little German boy brought a can of water and gave the men a drink. One of the men who was getting parcels from England gave the boy a large piece of chocolate, a thing that was very rarely seen in Germany since the war. The boy's mother was a lady of upper class, but went to the restaurant, bought some cigars and gave them to the men thanking them for giving chocolate to her boy. The people waved to us as we passed them through the station.

The only demonstration of ill-feeling during the whole of the journey was when passing a signal box a railwayman shook his fist at us as we went slowly by, and just to pull his leg, the boys waved to him in return and smiled. We passed through Hildesheim and then we lay down for the night, there being just room for us to lie full length in the carriage. Next morning we arrived at Halle at 5.30am and here again we all detrained and marched off into a large building and given some more soup. For those who wanted it there was coffee. Another train load of prisoners had pulled up

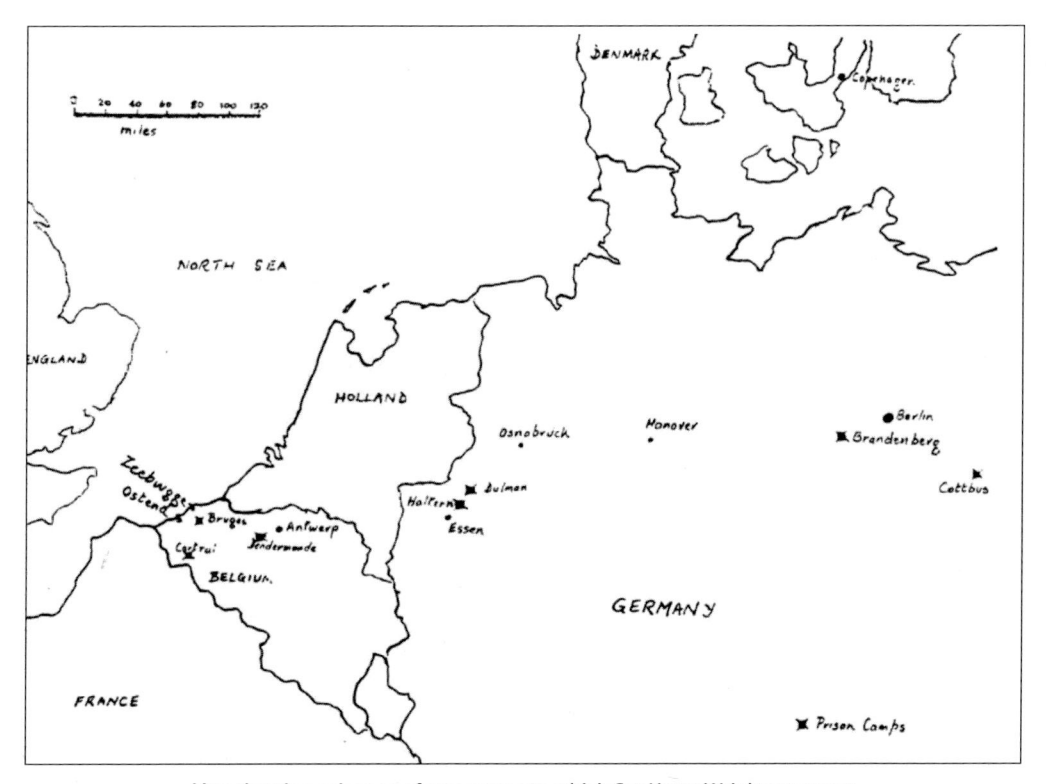

Map showing prisoner of war camps to which Sgt Harry Wright was sent.

behind us, these NCOs having been picked up from Munster and Sennelager camps and our number now totalled 2,000 NCOs. There was plenty of water about the station so we had a good wash and brush up and some of them had a shave. The girls working on the engines gave us hot water and those who could speak English told us about the war. They were of the opinion that it was impossible now for the Germans to win the war, but they hoped to make it a draw by no indemnities or annexations. The only men working on the trains were engine drivers, but the stokers and guards were women and they were dressed in railway uniform, breeches, leggings and jacket exactly like the men. There were women engine cleaners and porters, all of whom were very friendly. We left Halle at 10.30am and after passing through Torgau and Kalan, we finally arrived at Cottbus at 5.50pm on 22nd August.

Cottbus

Having been well fed from our emergency parcels, a good rest in the train and a chance to wash, we were looking fairly respectable as we detrained at Cottbus. It is a large town situated 80 miles SE of Berlin and has some fine buildings, also it was one of the cleanest towns I have been in. It is not often that townspeople have the opportunity of seeing 2,000 British NCOs march through their streets and the whole town turned out for the occasion. Thousands of people lined the streets but these were quite orderly. If we expected to see these people in a state of starvation we were sadly disappointed. They looked fairly well, dressed well and looked moderately happy. These people were not hostile towards us nor passed any comments. Some even showed signs of sympathy as our lads, in a bad state of health, went hobbling by in their wooden clogs. We heard afterwards that the German authorities had issued orders that as 2,000 British NCOs were passing through the town that evening, the town must look its best.

On the way to the camp we met some British soldiers who were working in the town. These men were looking very well and quite happy. They shouted across to us that they had been prisoners since 1914. It was three miles to the camp which was situated in the country. On our arrival we were marshalled into several groups, standing in columns of fours, and counted off in hundreds and separated. Each column of 100 men was now counted five or six times by two German Sergeants who counted out loud as they walked up and down the column. They would not take the 2,000 men over until they were quite certain that everyone was here. It was quite dark by the time they had finished.

We were now put together in groups of 400 and marched off to different compounds which had one huge hut surrounded by barbed wire. Outside this hut was a heap of dirty straw and a heap of dirty bed ticks. The lads went for the ticks and started filling them when someone shouted *"Don't touch that, you will get some clean straw tomorrow."* Some of us however took no notice of this order and made sure of one bed until we could get another, for the straw and bed ticks were cast away next morning and no more ever came. There was no light in the hut and everything was in inky darkness. At each end of the hut were rows of wooden beds fixed to the floor in two tiers. In the centre were eight long tables and stools. It had previously been used by Russian prisoners and they, no doubt being removed in a hurry, had no time to clean it out and left it in a filthy condition, dirt and rubbish all over the place.

We were given the usual two blankets, one bowl and spoon; and soup, the best I have ever tasted in Germany, was served out late that night. It consisted of thick barley, and the cook, a French Sergeant Major sent word round, that he was sorry the soup was not what it ought to be, but it would be much better in future. As a matter of fact, although I was in this camp six weeks, I never tasted any that equalled that first night, and after a day or so the usual story was going round they had not enough food to feed us properly, they did not know so many were coming or they would have got bigger stocks in. The railway traffic was held up so we must be on short rations. Indeed we did get short rations, but it was certainly better than the last camp, but not much.

The men who were captured in March in this case were unfortunate, for they had neither money nor food, and being hungry a concert would have cheered them up a little. They were left with the alternative of selling their few clothes or jewellery to get money or not go to the concerts at all. Money could be sent out from England through the International Money Exchange, but as none of us had yet received letters, we could not hope for money for some time. Our two friends treated us to the concerts and I had one or two very enjoyable nights there. A number of the comedians were men who were suffering the pangs of hunger, but they carried out their turns remarkably well. I doubt if any actor in the world sang or acted under such conditions as these lads did, hungry and miserable as they must have felt, and yet they stood there trying to cheer and make laugh their equally hungry comrades, a hunger that none of us will ever forget.

We were supposed to stand to attention if a German Sergeant passed us. One hot day some 40 or 50 of us were sitting on the grass near the canteen. It was very pleasant round there and we could see a little of the country. Some of us were reading, others talking and some sleeping. A German Sergeant came stalking round the corner and we did not notice him, but he soon let us know he was there. Like most Germans he started yelling at the top of his voice, saying something in German which no one understood and then started waving his arms about. We looked at the man and wondered if he had suddenly gone mad. Someone at last understood what he wanted and to save him drawing his sword which he seemed inclined to do, we all stood to attention. He then saluted us and passed on.

The YMCA church would only accommodate 100 men so we held our church services in the theatre. The German YMCA supplied the prayer books and we had morning and evening services each Sunday. We had two Sergeants in camp who preached in turn and I have rarely heard better sermons in any church in England. The theatre was always crowded and one had to go very early to get a seat. One Sergeant had been captured in March and as he stood there in his dirty clothing and wooden clogs, one could not help but admire him. He preached his sermons without notes, straight from the heart, telling us that his starvation was only a lesson from God and it taught us two things. That when we got back to England we must not be extravagant as we often are in the homeland, and also we should be more inclined to help others more unfortunate than ourselves. *"Bear in mind"* he said *"there were thousands in England suffering the pangs of hunger as you are suffering now. Quite a number of them were little children, did you help them?"* We also had a church service every Wednesday night and prayer meetings every day from 8.30 till 9am for the purpose of praying for the sick and wounded and the success of our arms.

There was an aviation school near the camp and we had them overhead every day. Very often we saw them come down out of control, two men being killed one day. These airmen did not seem as daring as ours. They never flew very high and the last bit of would keep them at home. The only planes that were high up was a patrol which came out regularly from Berlin looking for British planes which they were always expecting over the capital.

The German Sergeant in charge of our group was a nice old man, who had served a considerable time on the Western Front and was now suffering from shell shock. Asked one day if his revolver was loaded he replied by pulling it out of its holster and showing us that it was quite empty. We told him one day that we were covered with lice, and putting up his hands, he looked quite shocked but he reported the matter at once. We were now ordered to fall in outside bringing our few belongings with us and we were marched off to be fumigated. All our hair was clipped short again and some special preparation smeared on our bodies which burnt the hair off. In the meantime special parties were detailed off to give the hut a good disinfecting. On getting back we were sent round to another empty hut which had not been cleaned out and was very dirty. We spent one night in this hut and picked up as many fleas as we had lice before, and brought them round to our disinfected hut which by this time was quite dry.

The Germans put a message round the camp saying that if NCOs care to volunteer for work they could do so. Only a few did volunteer and these men had a rough time of it from their comrades. After we had been in the camp for seven weeks our emergency parcels arrived from Copenhagen and we were given one each the next day, and also six packets of Huntley and Palmers biscuits, but what pleased the boys most was that in each parcel were five packets of Wild Woodbines. If the people in England could have had one glance at these men's happy faces when they got their parcels, they would have been well rewarded for helping to subscribe towards them.

Amongst the NCOs in camp were school teachers and school masters, some of them holding the degree of BA. These fellows formed classes and taught the following subjects, German, French, Arithmetic, Grammar, Biography, History, Elementary Shorthand and the General Army Course. Quite a large number of us attended the classes. We had a Frenchman to teach us French and it was astonishing how quickly the men learnt it. An English Sergeant taught the German language.

We knew there was a camp at Brandenburg for naval prisoners of war and being Marines our interests are more with the Navy than the army. We were talking one day to a French sailor who had been there and he said it was quite a good camp. We talked it over and four of us decided to try and go to Brandenburg. I now wrote to the Commandant using as much soft soap as possible, for it goes a long way with the Germans and respectfully requested to be sent to Brandenburg Naval Camp as we were naval ratings captured off a ship. Two days later we were informed if we cared to pay our railway fares and that of our escort we could go. We measured the distance off a large map, found it was 100 miles from Cottbus to Brandenburg. Through enquiring we found we would travel at the army rate and it would cost each man 7marks, not including the sentries fare. To get the money was the next item as none of us had any money at all, but we did possess some woollen jerseys. We went round to the Russian Jews and after a lot of bartering, I sold mine for 11 marks and the others sold theirs for about the same price. Another request was now written to the Commandant informing him that we were willing to pay all expenses. We now had to await replies from Berlin.

On 26th September we were removed to a separate compound which was empty, given a good bath and our committee gave us an emergency parcel to take with us. We remained in this compound until 28th September when at 5am we were told to get our things ready and fall in. We were given one thin slice of bread and some very thin soup, and then accompanied by a sentry we proceeded to Cottbus station. We caught the 6.40 train en route for Berlin and we travelled 4th Class. The carriages however were quite good. *'Many a true word is spoken in jest'* is a very old saying. Three years previous to this I was counting over some ammunition when a German prisoner passing by asked me what I was going to do with all that pile, *"saving it"* I replied *"for when we march on Berlin."* "Yes" he said *"you'll go to Berlin alright but only as a prisoner,"* and his words had now come true.

Our sentry was one of those fellows who seemed tired of life. He certainly was fed up with the war according to his conversation. We breakfasted from our parcels, and the German soldier looked rather amazed as we pulled out some of the good things. Our sentry, like us, only had a piece of black bread to come away with. We changed at two stations, one being Johannisthal and finally reached Berlin at 11am. It was always one of my ambitions to go to Berlin and I had got there at last. The station was crowded and as we walked up the platform we expected a few sneers and sarcastic remarks but none were forthcoming. On the whole the German people treated us fairly well, some even smiled as we walked by. Our sentry left us on the platform and went to inquire about the trains, and then we had to cross the town to another station.

The next train left for Brandenburg at 3pm so this meant a wait for over three hours. Our sentry told us to follow him and he took us to a large restaurant and told us to sit down at a table and have our dinner. What a contrast to our restaurants at home. There was not a particle of food exhibited anywhere and the only things in the place were two urns of black coffee without any milk or sugar. The restaurant was crowded with soldiers and civilians and the latter especially looked war weary and miserable. There was not a smile on any of their faces. If ever a nation was sick of war Germany was. As the people came into the restaurant they brought their own food with them and ordered their coffee.

In was rather amusing to see an officer come in with a fashionably dressed lady who put her hand in her dress pocket and pulled out some slices of black bread smeared with grease. I have often wondered what people thought as we opened our parcels and exhibited corned beef, biscuits, cheese, dripping, etc. We did not wish to exhibit our food before starving people but we were hungry and there was no reason why we should not have a good dinner. We gave our sentry a good dinner too for he was kind to us. Had he wished he could have made us stand on the platform for three hours. On our left was a poor woman with two very thin children. To show our sympathy with the kiddies we gave them a handful of biscuits which we had plastered with dripping. So hungry was the woman that she took some of the biscuits off the children and ate them herself. I took a packet of Fry's cocoa to the counter and asked for some boiling water. Quite a murmur went round as I did this as cocoa is very scarce and costly in Germany. The girl brought it to our table when it was ready and we gave her some biscuits which she readily accepted. The manager of the restaurant came over to us and said in quite good English *"If German prisoners were going through London, your people would not give them boiling water and make their cocoa for them, and they are not treated so well as you fellows are treated by us."* We treated this little speech with a hearty laugh for it struck us as very funny. *"Have you ever been to England?"* I asked *"No"* he replied. *"Well"* I said *"It may interest you to know that on all the principal stations in England there are free buffets where soldiers get free cocoa, sandwiches and cake, and I can assure you that if German prisoners were going through London, they would be treated the same as British Tommies. Whilst in the camps they get exactly the same allowance of food as the British civilian."*

We went on to tell him about the good food we had in England just prior to being captured at Zeebrugge. At the mention of the last word he said something to the people in the restaurant and they gathered round to have a look at us. He then explained to us that the Zeebrugge raid was known throughout Germany as the bravest deed on record. They listened with interest to our explanation of the raid, the manager turning our conversation into German for the benefit of the others. The people got very friendly after this and many a smile and 'Goot Tag' we got afterwards as they left the restaurant. The manager brought a large plate of apples to give us and one of the men gave him some cocoa.

Our sentry who wanted something in town, left his loaded rifle under the table and left us. He came back one hour later. During his absence we strolled around the station and had we cared to go out in the town no-one would have troubled. At 2.30 we lined in the queue behind a barrier to catch the 3pm train. The queue was a mixture of gentry, middle class and very poor people, about 150 in number. Everyone was carrying their own packages, the only porters on the platform being very old men and young girls. All tickets and passports were examined by the military police at the barrier. Officers, soldiers and civilians all had to show their tickets. We shuffled through with the crowd and there was a general rush for the carriages.

The train was soon packed to overflowing, some of the people carrying crates of fowls and ducks and these went into the carriages with them. We were ordered to the end of the train where much to our surprise a special carriage was unlocked and we got in. The carriage was a large double one with accommodation for about 40 people. The door was locked as soon as we got in. As the train was soon full up, quite a number of people thumped on our carriage trying to gain admittance, but after a few heated remarks in German, they went away. The train left punctual to time leaving a good many disappointed people on the platform.

Some miles up the line, the carriage door was unlocked and 40 British sailors, guarded by two sentries, got into our carriage. After the usual handshakes, for they were very pleased to see us, they told us they had been prisoners for two years. Quite a number of them belonged to the destroyers *HMS Nestor* and *Nomad*. They were looking well and like all sailors were a jolly crowd of men. They called themselves the 'Forty Thieves'. Their jackets were loaded with potatoes and apples which they had taken from the fields. These men had been working on the railways laying rails and packing sleepers, and in their spare time robbing orchards, etc.

One of them passed the remark *"My word you fellows look bad, you must have been through it."* On being asked what kind of camp Brandenburg was they replied *"It's a rotten camp. Full of fleas and rats and known all over Germany as the worst prisoner of war camp in the country. Our government at home has their eye on it. One of our fellows was burnt to death at that camp. He tried to escape through the window but was bayonetted back into the flames." "But"* I replied *"we are used to fleas and rats. What is the food like there?" "Oh"* they replied *"the food is splendid. You don't touch the German food at all. You swop your black bread for potatoes and soup you never see. All the lads are getting their parcels regular from England and they'll stand by you when you arrive in camp. NCOs have a good time at Brandenburg as no-one worries you."* They next gave us some vivid descriptions of how sentries kept them at work by butting them with their rifles. *"Oh yes"* said one man *"the sentries get every ounce of work out of us whilst we are at it, but they shut their eyes to what we do at dinner times."*

These men were living in a shed in the town and not at the camp, so on arriving at the station of Brandenburg, they shook hands with us and marched off. Our sentry met a chum and after a long talk with him, he came back and informed us that it was about four miles to the camp but the trams went half way there. If we cared to pay the tram fare, which was 2d, we could ride on the tram. We boarded the tram which like the trains was overcrowded. The people in the tram looked white and ill, and had haggard expressions on their faces. They looked well-dressed but on closer examination the material was very poor and rumour has it that quite a lot of the dresses are made of paper. I certainly have not seen dresses similar to those in England.

Brandenberg

It is a magnificent town with very wide streets and beautiful buildings. There is a fine monument in bronze to Frederick the Great. A very old town, hundreds of years old with a large bronze tablet inscribed, to the memory of the Brandenburg troops who lost their lives in some big battle in the present war. There is also a stone statue of Roland standing 20 feet high with a huge sword in his right hand and a dagger in his left. These Roland monuments date back to 1119AD and a full description of them can be found in Encyclopaedia Britannica, written by T A Archer of Oxford. Brandenburg, being a military centre has also a huge barracks and Red Cross hospitals. The river Havel runs through the town.

There were plenty of things exhibited in the shop windows, especially jewellery, but like the smaller towns not a particle of food was to be seen anywhere. The tram took us to the end of the town and we started our two miles walk through the countryside. The fields on either side had potatoes growing, in fact potatoes were everywhere and seemed to be Germany's chief production.

We soon sighted the camp which like all the rest was wooden huts surrounded by barbed wire and boardings. This camp was used by the French prisoners in 1870 and was now occupied by British, French, Russians and Italians. The camp had about

Birds eye view of Brandenburg prisoner of war camp, 35 miles east of Berlin
(The handwriting in these photographs is Harry Wright's)

10,000 prisoners either in the camp or attached to it, and of this number 2,000 were British. The river Havel skirted the camp on one side and a large wood on the other. There was a small lake in the centre of the camp.

On getting to the camp a German Sergeant took us over and gave our sentry a receipt for us. We were now put in a low building which had evidently been used as a cow pen. Dirt and filth were on the floor and there were some wooden boards for us to lie on. It was quite dark when we got inside and it only had one small window a foot square covered with barbed wire. The door was locked and a sentry put outside with the usual loaded rifle and fixed bayonet. I measured this dirty hovel and it was 20 feet long by 15 feet wide. No food was given us that night and not even a drop of coffee for us to drink. So our day's rations for that day as far as the Germans were concerned was one thin slice of black bread. We asked permission to go to the latrine but this was not allowed. We had our suppers from our parcels and then lay down on the boards to sleep using our parcels as pillows. The rats, being tame, hungry and strong, kept us company that night and would have taken our parcels away wholesale had we not been laying on them.

Don't for a moment, dear reader, think we were depressed by our surroundings and conditions. Two of the lads started singing and the rats only amused us. The majority of us would sooner have rats for company than lice. We were given no breakfast next morning but at 9am we were taken across to the office where full particulars were taken about us. The orders of the camp were read out and we had to take our caps off, a thing which is unusual for any soldier to do even if he goes before his commanding officer. We were now told we must show our respects to German NCOs by taking off our caps and must always do so in future when coming before them. These reptiles were responsible for having us put into that stinking hovel and no food, and now we must show our respects to them.

We were now taken to a stores shed where we were given a wooden bed, paper mattresses which we filled with straw, two blankets, a bowl and a spoon. We now had orders to go to No 10 hut which was situated 500 yards away, so placing one bed on top of another we started to struggle along. Being in a very weak condition it was as much as we could do to lift them and much more to carry them, but some of our comrades quickly came to our assistance and carried our load for us. What a surprise awaited us. The room was a small one, just big enough to accommodate about 30 men and we just filled it. It was the most comfortable room we had lived in since our capture. Most of the men were Petty Officers of the Royal Navy. Their length of time as prisoners varied from 18 months to two years and having been in the same hut all the time they had decorated it up very nicely. All the walls were papered with white paper and pictures cut from magazines were hanging on the walls. Cupboards had been made from Red Cross package cases and everyone was in possession of cups, saucers and plates. In the centre of the room was a large stove and their dinners were cooking. Our comrades soon made room for us and asked what regiment we belonged to and on being told that we were Marines they were quite pleased, but on being told we were captured at Zeebrugge someone shouted to the others, and they all gathered round and wanted to know the full particulars. They informed us they only had the German version.

We told them everything. One of them said *"The Germans had denied the canal was blocked."* We now assured them we had seen the ships submerged in the canal, and by the aid of a pencil and paper showed how the ships were lying. The lads gave a cheer when they knew this. They asked how long we had been in camp and being told we arrived the night before and spent the night in the cow pen, they replied that it was the usual thing, but had they known they would have brought us round some hot drinks and blankets. They had to bribe the sentry to let them pass things through the window. All these men were in receipt of parcels and soon collected round and gave us a good breakfast.

We were taken over to the committee room and Sergeant Major Walker gave each of us an emergency parcel which he said must last a fortnight. These parcels would last, with care, for 10 days, but the other men in the room took good care we never had any more German soup, and Sergeant Major Walker would always stretch a point when we were in need. On getting back to the hut we were asked out to dinner and I dined with two POs and had the best dinner since my capture; it consisted of fried bacon, potatoes and beans, washed down with a bottle of beer and finishing with an English cigarette. I had not finished dinner long when one of the men asked me if I would like to mess in with him as he was getting his parcels regularly from England and had a good stock in hand. I explained how I was situated with one emergency

A group of English prisoners at Brandenburg camp in 1918

parcel a fortnight and no prospects of getting a parcel from England. *"Never mind that"* he said *"we'll manage very nicely,"* so I accepted the offer to share and share alike all the time we were in Germany. It is the usual thing for prisoners of war to mess in together. Usually two, three or four get together and when each man gets his parcel he puts it in the mess so if one man's parcels are held up for a month, which is often the case, he doesn't have to go back on German food.

That evening a concert was being held in the theatre and free seats were reserved for us right in front. It lasted from 7 till 10pm and was exceptionally good. The principal turn was a rake and scythe dance by 16 boys under 18 years of age captured off merchant ships. Eight of them dressed as girls and eight as boys. They were trained by a French instructor who also took the boys at gymnastics. At the concert there was a presentation to a Russian doctor by the English and Americans in recognition of his services in attending the sick during the last four years. This doctor, it is said, had done everything in his power to assist the various nationalities in the camp. In 1916 he must have been very busy for over 1,000 Russians lost their lives through typhoid. These men were allowed to lie about dead in the camp. The German doctors would have nothing to do with them and it was only through the Russian doctors volunteering to come from Russia and be interned as prisoners at Brandenburg that this terrible disaster was kept under control.

Up to this time only four Englishmen had lost their lives at Brandenburg. One had been shot in the mines; one had been fatally burned to death whilst in a cell; one had died of old age, and the other had been poisoned eating some bad corned beef. So this camp must be counted as one of the lucky ones as far as Englishmen were concerned. We soon got settled down at the camp and were quite comfortable. We only had to fall in once a day for muster at 6.30am and then the rest of the day we just did what we liked. Our committee soon kitted us up with plenty of underwear and gave each of us a good top coat. We were also given soap, etc, to keep ourselves clean.

There were about 1,000 Russian prisoners working in the camp and in the fields adjoining the camp. Quite a number of them were Jews and they acted up to their calling. Such things as potatoes, cabbages and carrots could be exchanged for our allowance of black bread. We could always get 12 large potatoes for a quarter of a loaf of black bread. The vegetables were brought in by the Russians working in the field. Those working in the towns would bring into camp cooking utensils, cups, saucers, etc, in fact anything you cared to ask them to bring. In exchange for these articles they wanted packets of tea, cocoa or biscuits, which they promptly took down to the town and sold it to the Germans at extortionate prices. No small quantities of dud tea found their way into German homes for the boys would carefully open their packets of tea, empty it into a basin, use it and save the tea leaves. They would dry the leaves on the stove and when filling the packet again, would put some good tea at the top and bottom prior to sealing it up. This dodge always worked successfully. It was different however with cocoa. A favourite trick was to fill the centre of the packet with cornflour, but some of the old birds who had been taken in had a habit of opening the packet and, much to our amusement, would put their finger down the centre of the packet and on withdrawing it would be brown and white, and of course not acceptable.

The German NCOs in the camp would often send the Russians round with potatoes etc, to barter with us. The Russians had to obey their orders, but would always tell us that the Germans had sent them round and we would have nothing to do with them, so their game was not successful. In the hut were lists of names in five groups and one group each went in turns to Brandenburg to fetch the parcels from the Post Office. A covered cart was used for this and pulled along with drag ropes. It was a fairly level road and 20 men were sufficient to drag the load of 300 parcels. We had the usual sentries always with us to see that no-one escaped. On getting to the Post Office, before each parcel was handed out, it was checked by the German postal authorities who took the name and number of the owner of the parcel and entered it in a book. Quite a number of parcels some days had been robbed and some of them had the contents removed and only just left the string and box. As our loaded cart went daily through the streets of Brandenburg all kinds of remarks would be made about the Englanders. Some of the people would smile and others would scowl. I don't think any of them believed their newspapers about England starving.

On getting the parcels to camp they would be taken over by the English Committee who would unload them into a store. The list of names would be taken of the owners of the parcels and one man would go round the huts and after shouting

Under their German guards, British prisoners fetch Red Cross food parcels from Brandenburg station, taking them back to their camp, where they were carefully collated and distributed

out the words *'War News'* would shout out the names. These men would next day go round to the package shed with blankets or boxes and as their names were called out, go in front of the counter with four Germans behind. These Germans would open the parcels and select a tin here and there and open it and cut the contents with a knife to see if there were any sketches or other information. After this investigation they would empty the contents into the blankets and keep the cardboard and string. All tins were gathered together by working parties, flattened out and loaded on to the trucks, and sent off to various factories. Some of the men, when going down to Brandenburg, would often put a few biscuits in their pockets to give to the children. Some of the little mites would follow the packet wagon through the town saying *'Biscuits Englander'* and some of the older men had little children of their own no doubt in England. It was possible to make a mistake sometimes however, for one day I offered a child a biscuit and she stuck her little head in the air and refused it, but another one I offered it to, who had no boots or stockings and was clothed in rags, readily accepted some biscuits and followed us up the road and wanted me to kiss her. The men liked going down with the wagon, and through being kind to their children, the people of the town were, with a few exceptions, kind to us.

We were not allowed in the shops but if any man wanted any particular thing it was always possible to get it through the townspeople. For instance I wanted a piece of china, a vase with the word Brandenburg on it. I asked a German official at the Post Office if he would get me one and he agreed. I told him I would come down with the wagon the next day and pay for it. I was quite a stranger to this man. For some reason I could not go down the next day so the German sent me three beautiful vases up to the camp by another man for me to choose one. I did not see him again for several days, and when I did I paid him for two and returned the other one to him. *"You trust the English then"* I said *"Oh yes"* he replied *"You English have been good to my little girl giving her chocolate and biscuits and I am only too happy to help you in return."*

We saw one day a company of Brandenburg soldiers just off to the front. They had the band with them playing some patriotic air, and their wives and children were in the ranks with them. These men were not by any means the pick of Germany's manhood; they were chiefly old men and boys and looked anything but fighting men. We were told that this was the last batch that was going to be sent from Brandenburg as it was now drawing to an end of hostilities. It was 10th October 1918. These men looked very unhappy and as I stood and watched them march by, I thought what a contrast to the 4th Royal Marines Battalion on their way to Deal Station, laughing and singing as if they were going on a picnic. I have often seen German troops off to the front and I can assure my readers that unlike the British Tommie they looked very unhappy indeed. One of the strictest punishments in the German army at home, if a man does anything wrong, is to send him to the Western Front at once.

The flu was raging at Brandenburg and we rarely went down to the town without seeing funerals. A German military funeral is similar to our own. The band is in front usually playing the Dead March from Saul, next comes the coffin carried by six German soldiers. The relatives follow on foot and about 20 German soldiers bring up the rear. There is no firing party. The coffin is covered with the Imperial Flag. Whenever we met these pathetic military funerals we would always halt with our wagon and show our respects by standing to attention and saluting which is customary in the British Army. I noticed however that the German soldiers passing any funeral paid no respects whatever. Germany of course is a cultured race but they certainly don't act up to it.

We had our own little church in camp. It was used by all denominations. Our preacher was a stoker captured off one of the merchant ships, who conducted services every Wednesday and Sunday nights. He was a good preacher and could do anything to help his comrades. He also conducted the services at the funerals during my stay at Brandenburg. One day I attended a funeral of a prisoner of war. He was a Newfoundlander named Bungay, captured off *SS Dictator*, a ship which had been sunk by a German submarine. Only 30 men were allowed to attend the funerals. We formed up at the mortuary and six men shouldered the coffin which was of the commonest wood without any paint. Preceding us was a seaman carrying a large wooden cross and following him was our stoker preacher, the coffin next and then a few mourners.

Surrounding us were the sentries with loaded rifles and fixed bayonets. The cemetery was outside the camp about one mile distant. On the way to the cemetery we passed German sentries guarding the camp. None of them paid any respects but farther up the road we passed a less cultured race of people, namely the Russians, who were working in the fields. These men at once stood to attention and took off their caps until we had passed them. After changing bearers several times we at last entered the churchyard gates and whilst we walked slowly to the grave, our preacher started the burial service and then we carried out the remainder of the service, standing around the open grave. After the service we sang a hymn and then our preacher gave us an address as we stood bare headed round the grave. The cross was put at the head and then some mourners were detailed to fill in the grave. Whilst this was being done the others walked round the graveyard. This cemetery specially for prisoners of war was very nicely kept. There were over a 1,000 wooden cross in memory of the Russians and in the centre was

Prisoners taking their midday meal in camp. The German ration usually consisted of one slice of black bread and two bowls of soup a day, though at Brandenburg the prisoners normally existed on food parcels.

a monument made of stone with a copper eagle on top with an inscription in the Russian language to the memory of the men who had lost their lives through typhoid at Brandenburg Camp in 1916. The Russian Jews were buried separate from the others and on top of the ground which I understand is their custom.

The four English graves were in good order. Each had a beautiful granite stone embossed with a huge anchor and the inscription, let into the stones, gold in colour. The stones, especially of the two men who had been murdered by the Germans must have cost a lot of money, money was unstintingly given by collections from British prisoners of war out of their meagre wages of 4d a day. We put two wreaths on the graves, the wreaths cost us £5 and worth about £2 in England, and then we marched back to camp and dismissed. The attendance at the funeral, which by the way was Church of England, was quite voluntary.

On 17th October there was a general inspection right throughout Germany for men to be sent to the front, and quite a number were picked from our sentries. The sentries now left to guard the camp were poor specimens of manhood. Weak boys wearing glasses, hardly strong enough to carry rifles, and even men of unsound mind, and others suffering from shell shock were seen walking about carrying loaded rifles. The Under Officers in charge of groups, although over 6 foot high, looked very ill. Their cheek bones protruding and yellow skins with their eyes sunk in their heads, it made one feel sorry for them, brutes as they were, I hardly think they had the strength to be cruel to us now. Those who could speak English would often come into our huts and tell us the war would soon be finished.

One of them one day passed a filthy remark about the iron cross he was wearing and none of them was very complimentary about the Kaiser. These fellows, when they could see the war would end to their disadvantage, became exceedingly nice to us. The huts were lit with electricity and we were supposed to put them out by 9pm. The sentries would come round and ask us very nicely to put them out, but if we gave them an English cigarette, we could keep them on all night, if we cared to.

Twelve months previous they would have enforced their orders with a few rifle shots or pricks of the bayonet. Having plenty of food at this camp we were quite happy. We would always be singing or skylarking. Very often a man who was too tired to get out of bed, would be carried bodily, bed as well, out of the hut into the middle of the camp and be left 300 yards away from the hut. Others would get their beds broken to pieces and everything thrown on top of the roof, and then when a poor fellow was almost mad with temper, we would set to and make him a new bed with odds and ends. We would often have a water fight when a few of us would get drenched to the skin. Windows would often be broken in our mad moments and those who had money would have to subscribe to have them repaired again.

In the centre of the hut the boards had been taken up and a huge hole scooped out where we secretly hid the coke which the Russians would steal off the Germans and bring to us in exchange for bread. All kinds of rumours were spread around the camp with regard to the war finishing and men would come to our hut with these rumours.

Without any warning half a dozen men would rush for the man of rumours and despite his struggles, would put him down the hole with the coke, put the boards on top again and sit on them for half an hour or so, and enjoy the man's oaths and bursts of temper coming from below. Warrant Officers were also subject to this treatment and would sometimes take part in the fun. The German sentries only looked on and laughed. We were known all over the camp as the 'mad hut'.

20 Petty Officers and NCOs were detailed by the Germans daily for work, such as working in the cookhouse and pickets on the latrines, but I never heard of anyone obeying the order and the Germans did not enforce it. During the winter month's white bread was sent to the camps from Copenhagen and each man was served with two large loaves each week. Our first supply came through on 1st November and we were very busy two days unloading the truck. Quite a number of starving German women and children saw us unloading but of course we could give one away. Six men slept in the truck all night to guard it from being robbed until we finished unloading the next day. The railway authorities in this case would not be responsible for our food supplies and our trucks previous to this had been robbed if they had to stay at the station one night.

A Russian in the camp translated the German papers into English each day writing the news into a book which was taken round the huts by an English Petty Officer and read to everyone. For this service we subscribed by giving the Russian food from our parcels that we could spare. *The Daily Mail*, a well-known London paper, could also be bought in Brandenburg for 1/-; it was about ten days old by the time we got it. A special prisoner of war paper was served out free once a month. Some of the men in camp could tell some interesting tales about their capture. There was a Marine there who had spent 17 days on a German submarine. Whilst aboard the submarine was chased by English destroyers who dropped depth charges. He described the effects as awful. The submarine rocked from side to side and nearly turned right over in the water. The German crew stuck to their post with white and haggard faces.

In the camp was a Warrant Officer who was taken off *SS Brussels*, Captain Fryatte's ship and he told us this pathetic tale. 'On being captured the Captain and his crew were put in Bruges convict prison in the same cell as we occupied. Whilst in the cell the Captain was repeatedly sent for by the German authorities to give an account of how and why he rammed the submarine. The Captain informed the others what was asked of him when he was put back in his cell, and passed a remark about the Germans intended making trouble. Soon afterwards the Captain and Mate were separated from the rest and put in a different cell. The Captain was now informed he would be tried by court martial for ramming a German submarine when ordered to stop. He was sent to Berlin for trial and as everyone knows he was sentenced to be shot. He was told one forenoon that he would be shot the following morning at 7am, and asked permission to write a farewell letter to his wife and children and was granted this request. At 6pm that night an escort came into the cell and informed the Captain that what they had told him that morning was a mistake and he was to be executed at 7pm that night, in one hour's time. Sometime before 7pm he was marched out to the back yard where a large firing party in charge of an officer was waiting. He was told to sit in a chair but as a last request he was not blindfolded. As it was quite dark and the yard badly lit, the officer shone an electric torch on the brave Captain's left breast and the firing party fired at the ring of light on a given signal from the officer. The officer, after the firing, drew his revolver and fired into the body of the Captain, which the officer always does at an execution. After the Captain's death, the German read the letter written by the Captain, but without any pity or even taking it to higher authority, this wretch tore it into fragments.'

I was grumbling one day because I had been a prisoner for six months and I had received no letters from home. A friend of mine, Mr E Buckingham, told me I should be luckier than him if I got one under 12 months. It appears that he was 3rd Officer in the Merchant Service and his ship the *SS Tumna* was sunk by the German raider *Wolfe*. He was taken aboard the *Wolfe* and was at sea dodging British men of war for over 12 months. They went round Singapore and Colombo laying mines. They hid round the Cocos Island and other out of the way places. She carried an aeroplane which she sent out in daytime to look for British Merchant ships. When she spotted one she would come back to the raider and report. The raider would then put to sea and sink the ship but not before taking her stores and crew. After 12 months at sea the raider got back safely to Germany with 360 British prisoners onboard, and not until they reached Germany were these men registered as prisoners of war.

Another man told an interesting tale about the German raider Mowe. This man was a seaman on the *SS Mount Temple,* a ship of 9,000tons and carrying a cargo of ammunition and 500 horses. One day they were surprised to see a merchant ship overtaking them and on drawing near fired a shot across *Mount Temple's* bows for her to stop. At the same time a German flag was unfurled and the side of the ship dropped down showing the supposed merchant ship to be bristling with guns. The *Mount Temple* was armed with one 4.7" gun and in reply to the order to stop, opened fire at once and fired 10 shots in rapid succession, nine of which struck the raider *Mowe* and she lay over to starboard. During this time the raider also was firing and killed two of the *Mount Temple's* crew and put the gun out of action. The men now took to the boats but the Captain refused to leave his ship and went down with her. To give an idea of how unevenly the ships were matched, the *Mowe* was armed with two 5"guns aft, two 6"guns for'ard and four torpedo tubes. She was also armed with machine guns which were worked by means of a wheel from the bridge. By turning this wheel the machine guns could be fired in any direction. She carried a complement of 200 men and during the action there were 400 British prisoners aboard. Throughout the action the *Mowe* was delayed 48 hours and her casualties were 28 men killed and 30 wounded. On getting aboard the *Mowe* the gunner was complimented by the Captain who patted him on the back and gave him a cigar. *"If all merchant ships were like you"* he said *"we would have been sunk long ago."*

After nearly six months I received my first parcel from England sent by the Navy

League and now, I thought, I shall get six a month like the other men. This parcel left England on 23rd August and reached me in good condition. This was however, the only one I ever had, the Germans must have had all the rest. Having been by this time six months a prisoner, I was very anxious to get news from home. We knew the flu was raging in England and our thoughts were always there. I had an idea there were letters in the camp but did not know how to get any of them. One night, however, I had a brain wave and sat down at once and wrote to the Red Cross at Copenhagen the following letter.

Dear Sir or Madam,

I am appealing to you to see if you can use your influence to have some letters forwarded on to me. I was captured at Zeebrugge 23.4.18 during the raid there, and up to the present I have received no letters or cards from home. I am married and during the last six months have been kept in awful suspense of waiting news from my wife to whom the report of my death would be made known directly my ship got home. My present address is Wyndham Place, Eldad Hill, Plymouth and any news of her present health, which I am afraid is not of the best, will be very welcome. I feel quite certain there are letters in this camp for me and they are being wantonly withheld from me by the German authorities. A word from you to the Commandant of the camp may be the means of having them released. Thanking you in anticipation.

I am yours obediently, Sgt H Wright.

I did not care if this letter never reached Copenhagen but one thing I did know, it had to pass the German censor who would then report me for writing such a letter. By a curious coincidence my letter was allowed to go through but before it had time to reach Copenhagen no less than 14 letters were handed to me by the Germans which goes to prove they were held up in camp. The Red Cross received my letter quite safe and at once cabled through to my wife and she was allowed to cable a reply free of charge. I am afraid we should have fared badly in Germany had it not been for these noble people of the Red Cross, who we could always appeal to in time of need.

The war news read out to us each night was particularly interesting and then at last the Armistice news began to leak out. We began to get excited, for our freedom was in sight at last, and only those who know what it is to be penned up behind barbed wire for months, and even years in some cases, can possibly understand what freedom meant to us. The 10th November was a memorable day for us. We already had news of the Kaiser's abdicating and the German sentries had come in our hut on the previous night and informed us that the next morning they were going to tear their ornaments out and everything that was a badge of military rule, and throw them away. When we had a roll call on the 10th November, the Under Officers in charge of us were still wearing their decorations, but the Senior Officer was not wearing his.

As each Under Officer went to report their group present, the Senior Officer gave them orders to take their decorations off. This they smilingly did at once. One would have thought that the Senior Officer would have used more tact than to give them the order in front of prisoners.

At 9am our senior Sergeant Major in camp went round the huts and informed us that members of the Soldiers and Workers Union were coming into camp during the day to address the German soldiers. He informed us a bloodless revolution had broken out all over Germany and the military rule smashed. He warned us to show no demonstrations and go quietly about the camp. The Germans had informed him that if we did they would not hesitate to do their worst to keep us in order.

In the vicinity of the camp was a tall building which had a commanding view of the camp. On top was a machine gun which could be brought to bear on any part of the camp. At 1045am, when members of the Soldiers and Workers Council arrived in the camp, the red flag was hoisted on top of this building. The Russians gave a hearty cheer but the Englishmen remained quiet. The representatives made for the General's house and he appeared at the door minus his decorations, shook hands with them and welcomed them to the camp.

During the day we had the Brandenburg papers which informed us that the carrier carrying the Armistice terms had not arrived at his destination and was still missing. We expected foul play and this cast a gloom over the camp. News came through later however that Field Marshall Foch had sent an aeroplane over with a fresh one. I went down to Brandenburg next day with the packet wagon. On all the main buildings

Brandenburg naval prisoners cooking their meals in the open air. Note the variety of clothing and headgear worn.

in the town the red flag was flying and in the main streets, lying on the ground, were hundreds of cap ornaments and shoulder straps, etc, which had been thrown away by the German soldiers. The officers and men were minus any of these badges and were wearing bits of red ribbon and red cap ornaments. Everywhere in the town we were met with happy faces, and nearly everyone shouted to us, "War finished Englander, go home to England".

We left the Post Office exactly at 11am when the length of time for signing the armistice was up. There were armed guards at the Post Office and station, and thousands of people all wearing red ribbon, stood around the streets. At 11am all the munition factories closed down and we met hundreds of work people making for the town. They waved to us as we passed and kept shouting in German to tell us to go home and not stop in the camp. One of the men had bought a paper in town and we read the terms of the armistice. We were No 13 on the list which was 'Unconditional surrender of all prisoners'. At 4pm that afternoon a small printed form was handed round the town to the people telling them definitely the armistice had been signed and there was great rejoicing in Brandenburg.

The English prisoners working in the factories and farms in the vicinity of the camp were brought in next day and we really thought the Germans were going to send us home quickly. On 14th November the representative of the Soldiers and Workers Council visited the camp for the purpose of addressing the prisoners. They were in civilian clothes and were of the middle class. We gathered round them and they addressed us as follows:

"We, the representatives of the Soldiers and Workers Council, greet the English and other prisoners in this camp. We ask you to forget and forgive all cruelties, etc, which have been committed during your stay in this country. Remember it was the military authorities and not the German people who made you suffer. We intend during the short time you are in this country, to do all in our power to make your lives as comfortable as possible. If you have any grievances you must come to us and we will remedy them."

Sergeant Major Walker asked them if all our letters which were held up in camp could be released. They replied they would be released at once and in future. Englishmen would be put in charge of all letters and we would get them on arrival in camp. In addition we could write as many letters home as we liked and they would not be censored. In reply to the question about Englishmen that were in convict prisons for civil offences, they said they would have them released at once. Quite a number of prisoners out working had been punished by having their parcels stopped. This, they said, would be looked into and the men would get all their parcels in future.

What every one of us wanted to know most was when we are going home. This question puzzled them somewhat, but they replied after some consideration *"We do not know, but it will be sooner than you think."* (Laughter) and when we did go home they hoped we would go in an orderly manner for some of the German population were very funny and may cause trouble.

The German papers next day had the following article. *"Any prisoner who cared to stay in Germany would be allowed to do so after peace was signed."* This gave us to understand that we would not be going home until after peace was signed and Armistice Term No 13 said 'unconditional surrender of prisoners at once'. We put this question before the Soldiers and Workers Committee and they informed us that what the German papers said was quite true and we should not leave the country until after peace was signed.

The men who were brought in off the farms and factories were now ordered to go back to work again. Some of the men refused but there was no sign of cruelty to make them go. After threatening to stop their parcels and starve them, the men agreed to work in reliefs by companies. The German papers commented on this in the following article: *"If British prisoners refuse to work, their nourishment will be stopped, but on the other hand, if they work, they will get the same pay as the German workman".*

The council came into camp one day and informed us that an agreement had been made between the German and English governments that our lads should continue to work down the coal mines until German troops could be brought from the front line to relieve them. Another article in the German papers on 16th November informed us that the question of prisoners meant that men in jail would be allowed to stay in the country after peace was signed and other prisoners would leave the country as soon as trains could be got to convey us home. This put us in better spirits, for the country being in a state of revolution, we did not feel very safe and were very anxious to get out of it. We also heard rumours that in some of our camps the mob had thrown the gates open and told the prisoners to go, and when they attempted to, they had been mown down by machine gun fire. Others, we heard, had broken out of camps and attempted to march 200 miles to the border and some had died by the roadside. The Germans informed us that, if we attempted to break away, they would not be responsible, and any bad conduct in the camp would be punished by clearing the camp last; and as there were 364 prisoner of war camps in Germany, we would wait a long time, so we decided to wait.

On 22nd November we had the misfortune to lose another Englishman named Horace Rapley, a seaman in the Royal Navy. He had been out at work and being ill, had been sent in. He now contracted double pneumonia and despite every effort to save him he died leaving a wife and three children. He was buried on 24th November and this time a photo was taken of the funeral party and the grave. A collection was made for his tombstone and that of Bungay's and over 2,000 marks was raised, the money being left to the care of the Red Cross who will see the tombstones are put up.

Notices were stuck up all over the camp saying how sorry the Germans were for the ill treatment of prisoners and yet on the commander's orders English prisoners were kept in ignorance that there was such a thing as an armistice. When these men did find out they refused to work. They were kicked and knocked about and in a good many cases still refused to work. They were put in prison and kept there. The Sergeant Major sent a sharp protest to the council about this treatment and asked for the men to be sent in. He also reported the terrible condition of some of the men who had deserted their work and come into the camp. They were not getting the civilian pay promised by the Germans. The council promised to do all in their power, but three weeks after this, the deserters came in with terrible tales of brutality and men were still being kept in prison.

Funeral of Prisoner of War at Brandenburg

The funeral of Able Seaman Horace *Bungay at Brandenburg. Only four British prisoners died there, but over 1,000 Russians had perished during the Typhoid epidemic of 1916.
(*Editor's Note: I believe this should read Horace Rapley. See paragraph above.)

On 22nd November 350 Merchant Seamen left the camp for England. At First 400 were told off but, just before leaving, the 1918 prisoners were told to fall out. The train that took them to their destination was not half filled when these men entrained at Brandenburg and could easily have taken 1,000 and yet the Germans were grumbling about the English not leaving them enough rolling stock to get the prisoners out of the country. It was a sad party for a good many of us for friends in a German prison camp are true friends. Most of us sent letters to England by these men and did not forget to tell them the truth this time.

At roll call one morning the German Sergeant Major informed us the Soldiers and Workers Committee invited us to Berlin where we would be addressed by an English officer and an Ambassador. A special train would be put at our disposal and they hoped all English, which numbered 1,000, would avail themselves of this splendid opportunity. Of course we all volunteered on the spur of the moment, but after we had argued the thing out about marching under the Red Flag, cinematograph shows being taken of us and sent to England, or perhaps be mown down by machine guns by people who did not like the khaki, there were only seven men left out of 1,000 who wished to go to Berlin. The Germans would not use a special train for seven men, so no one went from Brandenburg. A few Englishmen did however go from other camps and an account of the meeting was published in German newspapers.

The general idea of the meeting was to ask the British prisoner on getting back to England to spread the report about the news of the German revolution, how it started and how easily the military power was stamped out; and to spread a good impression about the new government; and to tell their friends at home that it was not the people's fault they had been brutally treated but that of the late military government which had just been kicked out. This was quite enough for our lads. Since arguments started between them and the Germans when they started speaking, there was such an uproar, they were obliged to close the meeting and march our fellows back to camp.

On 25th November some very cold weather set in and we were able to go skating on the lake. This relieved the monotony for a time. Ice skates had been bought a year before and there were plenty of them lying about in the camp so we had a splendid time while the cold weather lasted. On 2nd December a representative of the Danish Red Cross came into camp, a Captain in the Danish Army. After inspecting our quarters he got us together and gave us a speech in English. He said the Germans were hit very hard by the Armistice terms. The English had demanded a large percentage of their rolling stock and they had very few trains at their disposal for the removal of prisoners. They hoped to get 25,000 prisoners out of Germany through the Baltic ports before Xmas. *"You must bear in mind"*, he said, *"that the seas are covered with mines and passages have to be swept and that all takes time. I have left Denmark with the invitation of not going back there again until the last British prisoner is out of Germany, so have patience, men, and we will get you out as soon as possible."* 97,000 parcels would arrive in Germany to be distributed out to the men going home and he assured us, we would be well looked after. He was well aware that the trains were being held up in Germany and our parcels stolen by the hungry German people, but the new German government had promised him in future that armed guards would travel on the trains and protect the Red Cross stores.

He invited questions and some of the men told him it was a lot of bunkum about the Germans being short of railway traffic. They could put a train at our disposal to go to a meeting in Berlin. Another man said if we do not get sent from here soon we will march out of the camp and find our way to the frontier. The Danish Captain replied *"If you do, you will starve by the roadside like others are doing."* "Yes" said one man *"We might just as well die of starvation on our way to the frontier as die in this miserable camp."* The Captain promised to see that a good supply of food was sent through to us and said he knew it was very trying for us but hoped we would have patience.

In a day or two after this an Ambassador came down to us and explained that the camps who gave the most trouble would be left till last, but promised to get all the men in from work and to do what he could to help us. Like the Captain he invited questions but now each man separately in a room. We picked our leaders out to explain our case and they saw the Ambassador. These men were so wild at being put off for so long and getting very short of food in camp, they were not very particular what they said to him and threatened all kinds of things if we were not removed very shortly. The Ambassador, white with passion, informed the men he would report them to the British government and, without waiting to see any more, he abruptly left the camp.

We had been three weeks without parcels and were getting very low when large stores arrived from Copenhagen, and I think I am safe in saying that the stores they sent would have lasted us three months without economising. We could do nothing more now but make the best of things and wait. We subscribed for two gold watches and presented one to the Chief Petty Officer who read the war news out every night, and the other we gave to a Private named Williams of some Canadian Regiment. It was through the untiring efforts of this man that many an English prisoner owed his life. Many a night this man had sat by a sick bed attending to his patients' wants and doing everything in his npower to get them well again, working of course on cooperation with the Russian doctor.

When we finally left for home one Englishman was very seriously ill and Private Williams volunteered to stay behind and nurse him. They were the only two Englishmen left there. I only hope the noble sacrifice of this man will be recognised when he gets back to his homeland. No one knows but the man himself what it meant to be left behind when everyone of his comrades was going home. The sick man was not told we were leaving.

So many men each day were allowed to leave the camp accompanied by two German sentries. I often went out with a friend. Some 60 of us would be by the gate each afternoon at 2pm and after being checked would leave the camp. It was always possible to get away from our sentries and this we often did and had a stroll around the town or country. A packet of biscuits was always enough to bribe any of the German guards round the camp if you wished to get out that way.

Whilst in town one day we were stopped by a German Petty Officer of the German Navy. He spoke very good English and asked when we were going home. He went on to say that he had served on the Western Front a considerable time and was also at Zeebrugge during that operation. He was quite surprised when I told him I was captured there. I asked him various questions about it. He replied by saying that now the war was over he need not be afraid of telling the truth. *"We did not"* he said *"know anything about you coming. We were all fast asleep with the exception of those on watch."* I asked what their casualties were and he replied 18 killed at Zeebrugge and he was not certain whether it was 10 or 12 killed at Ostend. The canal, according to his idea was effectively blocked at Zeebrugge but not at Ostend until the *Vindictive* came a second time and sank herself. He told us the ships were heeled over on their sides and a passage made for the submarines to go to sea in a fortnight after they were sank, but he continued that it was never really successful because of the sand drifting in the channel. No less than 22 bodies were washed ashore next day at Zeebrugge, and together with those washed up on the Mole, were buried with full military honours. We expected you to make a general landing at Zeebrugge so troops with heavy guns were withdrawn from the Western Front to man the Zeebrugge and Ostend defences and also strengthened the barbed wire entanglements. Quite a number of decorations were given to officers and men by the Kaiser when he visited the scene. The whole of the German Navy admired our pluck, he said and *"we should not have done a greater thing had we landed on Dover pier."* *"Oh yes"* he replied in answer to a question of mine about the revolution, *"We in the Navy started it. Our government wanted us to go to sea and meet your fleet, and of course we refused. We knew we should not stand much of a chance in a sea fight and our refusal was the means of starting the revolution which ended the war. I wish I was in England again"* he said and wishing us goodbye and good luck, he left us.

On 17th December my friend and I went down to Brandenburg for the last time. We had given our sentry to understand that we would wait for him at the entrance to the town and as he did not seem to mind whether we did or did not, we went into town by ourselves. We had not gone far before we met over 100 schoolchildren each one of them carrying a large black, white and red flag, and all singing some patriotic song. They marched some distance past us and then lined each side of the street. On getting further into the town we found the streets lined with thousands of people and mounted soldiers keeping them in order. All the houses were decorated with bunting flags of all description, the red flag being the most conspicuous. Thinking the town was in a state of revolution we were about to beat a hasty retreat back to camp, when we saw a German soldier and decided to ask him what was the cause of all the excitement. He replied in German, that all the Brandenburg Regiments were that day returning from the Western Front and the town turned out to welcome them. We decided, after some hesitation, to run the risk and mix with the crowds.

On getting to the centre of the town the crowds were so dense we were about to move on when a wagon and two horses, which had pushed through the crowd and could go no further, stopped right by us. Up we jumped into the wagon and also some Germans. The horses were very lively and few people dared get into the wagon so we had plenty of room. We now had a splendid view. A clear open space was allowed for the troops to pass and mounted police and soldiers kept the crowd well in hand. The Brandenburg Regiments headed by a strong military band were just then coming up the town. The General was a fine type of German manhood wearing many decorations and looking quite pleased, and then came the troops, some 10,000 of them, with their officers and military bands. The officers looked very smart in their uniforms and they were well mounted. Most of them were carrying bunches of flowers and their horses were also decorated with flowers. The troops, of which I took particular notice, looked remarkably well. As they went swinging by, all in step, one could not help but admire them. These men were strong, well equipped and smart. Whatever the German population may have suffered by lack of food, these men had not been neglected and they looked a different race of people entirely to the civilians.

We were conspicuous by our khaki as we stood up in the wagon and some of the German soldiers saw us as they went by. These men smiled and shouted *"Hello Tommie,"* but the officers who were attracted to us by the men shouting, looked none too pleased and seemed to resent us being there. I only saw two guns in the procession and they were rather small ones. The transport, chiefly field kitchens, brought up the rear. The people cheered them certainly, but it was a half hearted cheer. It put me in mind of someone crying and cheering at the same time. I hope when our lads come home from the front, the crowds will cheer better than that or not cheer at all. If ever I felt proud of being an Englishman it was while watching this defeated and brutal army march back to their homes.

After marching through the town they were finally taken to their barracks. There was no demonstration of ill feeling towards us as we intermingled with the crowds, but we heard all kinds of remarks about Englanders as we passed by. One old lady did give me a push but I only smiled in return which seemed to please her. One must be on their best behaviour when intermixing with an enemy crowd on such an occasion as this. A German Sergeant stopped us in the town and spoke to us in quite good English. For the sake of having something to say I asked him where he learnt our language. *"Why"* he replied *"I have just returned from England. I was a prisoner there for two years and then got exchanged."* I asked him how he liked England and he replied *"Very well, I got better food than I could ever hope to get in Germany."* I had seen an Iron Cross exhibited in a jeweller's window and I asked him if he would buy it for me to take back to England as a curio. He agreed and bought it for me. He now asked us to spend the evening with him at his expense but we declined, saying we had to be back in camp by 7pm, so we made our way back to camp. Some of the Germans in the town promised the prisoners they would take them to the Western Front for 300 marks by motor car. The prisoners must be in civilian clothes and supply the food for the journey. Two sailors availed themselves of this opportunity.

News suddenly came through that we would leave Brandenburg for home on the 18th December at 11am, so on the 17th we celebrated the occasion by having an all night concert and thoroughly enjoying ourselves. We gave all our personal stocks of food away to the Russians, French and Italians remaining behind, keeping just enough for the railway journey. On the 18th we were told it was cancelled till the 19th but food for that day was soon forthcoming from the committee which thanks to Sergeant Major Walker RE was full up to the last minute of our departure and to be turned over to our allies as soon as we left.

The Germans passed orders round telling us to take plenty of food for the railway journey and also we could take one of their blankets. We returned our bedding, bowl and spoon, and all our personal effects which our allies did not want, we smashed up so the Germans should not have them. We fell in to be mustered at 11am, standing separately from the others as our names were called. Two Italians, dressed in British sailors' uniforms, answered the names of the two men who had gone to the Western Front by motor car. There was a little Russian boy 14 years of age, who we used to feed and care for. This boy wanted to come with us and by some means he was smuggled out of camp. One of our pet cats (the other two were picked up and eaten by the Russians) was also taken with us. Most of us shook hands with Private Williams who stood at the gate to watch us go.

A special train was in the station for us and we soon entrained. The Commandant of the camp was on the station to see us off as the train left at 1.30pm. About ten miles up the line we were shunted on to a siding, our engine taken off and there we remained for nine hours. In the compartment where I was one man was very ill. The doctor advised him to remain behind but he refused saying he had quite enough of Germany and wanted to get home. We started again just after 10pm, the train going very slow and finally stopped at a big station where men who required it could have soup. Not many wanted it. One man was put on a stretcher and taken to the hospital at this station. Our next long stay was in the country where we detrained and decorated our train with firs, cabbages, carrots, etc, and some of the men in possession of black bread attached a piece of string to it and by means of a stick fixed it to the top of the carriages. When the train started again it was almost impossible to see any part of the train for vegetable leaves and firs, and notices written by the men were not very complimentary to the Germans.

Two cards had been given to us to fill in and these were to be handed in when boarding the steamer. We arrived at Warnemünde at 4pm on 20th December and alongside the wall were three Danish ships waiting for us. Our names were called out alphabetically and as each man went up the gangway he handed in his card. It was quite dark by this time and as we did not wish to leave the Russian boy behind, some of the men that had gone on board lowered a rope over the bows of the ship. We on shore, tied the Russian boy to it and he was hauled inboard. Whilst I was waiting for my name to be called a German sailor came to me and asked me if I had any white bread I could give him as he had not seen any for a long time. I am afraid I was not very gracious in replying in the negative.

About 6pm the last man was on board and we were then free men once more and no one knows but prisoners what that feeling was like. It was only a small ship and there was not much accommodation but we did not mind that. A good hot meal was served out to us at once with a bottle of beer and apples. Owing to the mines not being cleared we had to wait until next morning before we could put to sea. We held a concert on board that night and had a very enjoyable time. The ship left Warnemünde at 6'30am next day. It was a rough passage and the majority of the men did not want all the nice things offered them to eat.

We went right alongside the wall at Copenhagen and a double decked train was waiting for us. We were marshalled into the carriages by Danish policemen and locked in. The train left at 6pm and after one hour's ride we arrived at a little station called Sandholm. We now had a four mile walk through the snow to the army barracks, led there by one of our officers who had come to meet the train. Motor lorries met the train for our luggage and anyone too weak to walk. On getting to the barracks we formed up in the square and were addressed by the Commandant in English as follows: *"Englishmen, I give you a hearty welcome to Denmark in the name of the Danish government. We all know only too well in this country the terrible suffering you have endured at the hands of a most brutal enemy. Forget what you have been through and enjoy yourselves while you are staying in this country. We shall do everything in our power to make you happy for a day or two until a ship is ready to take you home. I need hardly ask you to conduct yourselves in a proper manner because as Englishmen, I know you will. Again I heartily welcome you."* We gave him three hearty British cheers and then we were marched off to our quarters.

The men were placed 20 to a room and four NCO's in a room. Everything was spotlessly clean. Each man had a nice comfortable bed with three very thick blankets and snowy white sheets and pillows. There were stoves in each room and we had an unlimited supply of coal and wood. The scenery from the windows was most magnificent and it was like being in heaven. There was a special building for the men to have their food, which was very good and there was plenty of it. The Petty Officers and Sergeants went to the Danish Sergeants Mess which was decorated with Danish and English flags. The rooms had comfortable armchairs. There were all the latest English magazines and papers and a piano. We sat down to our meals with the Danes and were attended to by waiters. Serviettes were always on the table for us to protect our dirty rags which we were then wearing. The food was the very best and cigars and wines were served out afterwards.

We were put into quarantine for 24 hours and after that we could go just where we liked. Christmas Eve was kept up by a concert which finished at 1am in the morning, and Xmas day we had everything we could possibly wish for. Xmas afternoon five of us went for a walk into the country and every child we met on the road saluted us and smiled a welcome. We were just passing a large house in the country when a gentleman came to the door and beckoned us in. We went into a cosy room and he served out cigars to us. He could converse in German and we got on very nicely. The lady of the house played English tunes on the piano and then we were given a good tea. We then left with many good wishes from our host as we had to get back for dinner. Each of us were given a big handful of cigars before we left his house.

On Boxing Day we were handed white sheets of paper to fill in to be handed on board at 11am we fell in ready for leaving the barracks for home. The Commandant thanked us for behaving ourselves and wished us a safe voyage. He also informed us that one of our comrades was in a critical condition in hospital. This was the man who had refused to stay behind in Brandenburg. The villagers turned out to give us a good send off and we boarded the train for Copenhagen.

There were thousands of Danish people on the quay when we arrived and alongside the wall was a large Danish American liner, the *Frederic V111* waiting for us. Each man showed his white paper as they went on board and was given a ticket with the number of his cabin on it. The little Russian boy was stopped on the gangway and it seemed likely that he would not be allowed on board, but after a considerable time he passed the danger zone and came on board. As he did so the officials were rather surprised at the tremendous cheer that went up from the Brandenberg prisoners. The Danish band played English tunes on the quay and the men that still had their ornaments threw them to the Danish girls as curios.

The ship left Copenhagen at 4.30pm that afternoon. The band played "Rolling Home to Merry England" as we left the quay and the Danes gave us a mighty cheer to which we responded. I think everyone on board that ship will remember the happy few days they spent in Denmark, and quite a number of the men remarked to me that they were sorry they were leaving Denmark although they were going back to England. These good people, right up to the time of our departure, did everything in their power to make our lives happy, and if any Englishman did not enjoy himself in Denmark it was not the fault of the Danes.

We anchored outside the harbour till next morning and then put to sea. There were 1,500 prisoners of war on board and nearly every man was allotted a cabin. The food was very good and plenty of it. Tobacco and cigarettes were also served out together with beer and spirits for those who cared for it. We had concerts on board also, and amongst the 1,500 men, we found some excellent talent. We had rough weather on getting two days out and 50% of the men remained in their cabins for obvious reasons. We were stopped one night by a trawler which had got into difficulties and the men, six in number, asked to be taken on board. These men were in a bad state when picked up and were floating about in the ocean out of control in a rough sea. One of them died before we reached England.

We dropped anchor at the mouth of the Humber at 1.45pm on 29th December. All the steamboats, destroyers and vessels in the vicinity used their sirens to welcome us, making signals 'Welcome home', etc. We were taken on a large tug up the Humber to Hull next morning, where before landing, a letter was read over to us from HM the King welcoming us home. As each man got on shore he was given a mug of coffee and a bag of food, and then got into the special train waiting in the station. Ladies came into the carriages and gave us cigarettes and postcards, the latter we wrote on and handed them back to the ladies who posted them to our people.

Amidst cheers from the crowds who came to welcome us, we left for Ripon in Yorkshire. At the station there were enough motor lorries to take us all into camp which was only a mile away from the station. We were given a hot meal that night and a clean bed to lie on. Papers were served out for the men to fill in, stating how they had been treated in Germany and mentioning names of any German who had committed murder or other acts of brutality. The paper also had the following printed questions:

> Do you know any man who had given information to the enemy, either voluntarily or through being forced by ill treatment?
>
> Do you know the name of any man who has done anything for the benefit of his country or comrades?
>
> State the name of any German commander in charge of an establishment who was responsible for ill treatment of prisoners, etc. etc.

Most of the Brandenburg men mentioned Private Williams. We were told by a gentleman who addressed us that any German who had been guilty of murder and ill treatment would be brought to trial, and the only way of getting information was through returning prisoners.

Next day we were sorted out into our own regiments and taken round to the various offices where full particulars were taken, medical examinations given by the doctors and we were finally kitted up. Each man was given a complete outfit in clothes and his other disgusting rags he was told to take off and put in a huge pile in the centre of the yard.

Early next morning, 1st January 1919, we were given a sum of money, ration cards, a free railway voucher to our homes and from there to our depots; also two half fare

BRANDENBERG

railway vouchers to travel anywhere at reduced fare during the holiday and a two months holiday. Special trains were in the station to conduct us north, south, east and west, and so we left for our homes and civilisation once more, after all the hardships and trying times the majority had undergone during their stay in Germany as prisoners of war.

I am indebted to the Royal Marines Museum, where the original diaries are preserved, for most of the photographs. Others have been taken from 'The World War 1914-1918 in Pictures' published by Amalgamated Press.

A drawing by Captain J S Hicks RM of the landing by the 4th Battalion on the Zeebrugge Mole on St George's Day 1918. This picture comes from the Royal Marines Corps Album published in 1932.

For further reading:

Zeebrugge *by Barry Pitt (Cassell – 1958)*
The Zeebrugge Raid *by Philip Warner (William Kimber – 1978)*
The Glory of Zeebrugge *by J Keble Bell (Chatto & Windus 1918)*
The Naval Memoirs of Sir Roger Keyes *(Thornton Butterworth Ltd)*
Roger Keyes *by C Aspinall–Oglander (Hogarth Press)*